HIKES
of Eastern Newfoundland

MARY SMYTH and
FRED HOLLINGSHURST

BOULDER
BOOKS

Library and Archives Canada Cataloguing in Publication

Smyth, Mary, 1953-, author
    Hikes of eastern Newfoundland / Mary Smyth, Fred Hollingshurst. -- Second
edition.

Includes bibliographical references and index.
ISBN 978-1-927099-72-8 (paperback)

    1. Hiking--Newfoundland and Labrador--Avalon Peninsula--Guidebooks.
2. Hiking--Newfoundland and Labrador--Bonavista Peninsula--Guidebooks.
3. Hiking--Newfoundland and Labrador--Trinity Bay--Guidebooks. 4. Trails--
Newfoundland and Labrador--Avalon Peninsula--Guidebooks. 5. Trails--
Newfoundland and Labrador--Bonavista Peninsula--Guidebooks. 6. Trails--
Newfoundland and Labrador--Trinity Bay--Guidebooks. 7. Newfoundland
and Labrador--Guidebooks. I. Hollingshurst, Fred, author II. Title.

GV199.44.C22N48 2016   796.5109718   C2016-900417-1

Published by Boulder Books
Portugal Cove-St. Philip's, Newfoundland and Labrador
www.boulderbooks.ca

Reprinted 2023

Editor: Stephanie Porter
Copy editor: Iona Bulgin
Design and layout: John Andrews

Printed in China

 We acknowledge the financial support of the Government of
Newfoundland Newfoundland and Labrador through the Department of Tourism,
Labrador Culture, Arts and Recreation.

Table of Contents

Trails by Region

Acknowledgments

When writing a book of this nature, you encounter many people who are helpful and full of encouragement in one way or another. We are grateful to all those kind people, but there are always some who deserve a special mention.

First, we would like to thank Ramona Dearing for planting the seed in us to try another hiking book and for suggesting we contact Gavin Will of Boulder Publications. Gavin and Stephanie Porter have been invaluable in helping us see the light at the end of the tunnel of information we have gathered to produce this book.

Neil Hardy and Sharon Collett provided a place to stay and information about the trails on Change Islands. Fraser Carpenter walked some of the trails with us on Fogo Island and provided a place to stay as well as her professional insights into nature viewing in the area. Fred Bridger was our guide for several of the Twillingate trails. Zita Cobb of the Shorefast Foundation and Cathy Crotty also deserve many thanks for their help while we were in Joe Batt's Arm.

Charlie Elton, a long-time hiking companion, helped considerably with hikes on the Bonavista Peninsula. Thanks also to Geralyn Christmas.

David and Lynn Smyth provided transportation and accommodations on the Bonavista Peninsula. David was also our long-suffering partner on the Old Trails near Eastport. John and Ros Smyth gave us a place to stay and introduced us to the Hant's Harbour-New Chelsea leg of the d'Iberville Trail.

Joe and Val Earles walked with us in Northern Bay and provided a healthy dose of hospitality after the hikes.

Ed Delaney has been a constant source of information and showed us the newly developed Cripple Cove Path on the East Coast Trail. East Coast Trail Association (ECTA) president Randy Murphy has also been very supportive.

Others who provided helpful information about the Centre Hill Trail, d'Iberville Trail, and the Old Trails include Yvette Mahaney, Robert Snook, Linda Pelley, and Susan Khaladkar.

Thanks also to those who have inspired and hiked with us over the years, including members of the Hiking and Adventure Club, Jim and Maxine Smyth and Frank and Anne-Marie Smyth, Paula Smyth, Garry Smyth and Egle Lorenzin, Chris and Mitzi Smyth, and Elizabeth Smyth-Boyle for the phone talks. Thanks also to Fred's sisters Ruth Norton and Phyllis Donnelly, our long-distance hiking companions. To all those others who wished us success and gave us encouragement along the way, we thank you.

To our children: Mary would especially like to thank her daughters Shannon and Tessa for their advice, wit, and irreverent humour in the process of writing and compiling this book. Ik hou van jullie. Fred thanks Amelia and David for being constant companions along every trail … sometimes in person, always in spirit.

Introduction

Is there anything that is better
than to be out, walking, in the clean air?

—*Thomas A. Clarke, Glennock, Scotland*

Convincing seasoned hikers of the benefits of a walk on a breathtaking coastal trail is like preaching to the converted. But for those just discovering hiking, we hope the joy of the activity and appreciation of the natural environment of eastern Newfoundland will make converts of you, too.

Exercise is part of it, of course. It is true you will get a workout from a visit to the gym, but the gym can never give you a wilderness environment with spectacular views of cliffs, beaches, wetlands, woodlands, and wildlife—with the smell of the salt sea air thrown in for good measure.

In our modern, increasingly urbanized world, it is easy to overlook our need for the natural environment and the physical, psychological, and social benefits it provides. But those benefits are real, and the trails in this book can make those experiences available to almost everyone.

This book features many of our favourite trails in eastern Newfoundland. Visitors to the different areas profiled will find additional trails worth exploring, and new ones are being opened up and developed all the time.

We encourage hikers who would like to try longer hikes and more challenging experiences on the west coast of the province to purchase *Hikes of Western Newfoundland*, also published by Boulder Publications.

The possibility of discovery is one of the great pleasures of hiking. There is no better way to enjoy the beauties of the natural world than on foot.

Newfoundland and Labrador, at the eastern
edge of Canada, borders the Atlantic Ocean.

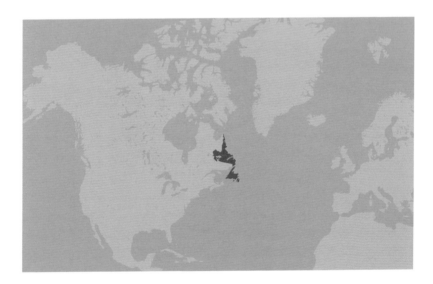

How to use this book

This book will give you the information you need to successfully get to the start and end of 86 of eastern Newfoundland's most spectacular hikes. The hike descriptions have been organized to be user-friendly, instructive, and, we hope, inspiring. Each hike is described in detail on a 2- or 4-page spread.

Page Layout

Nearest community/town name (or park or route number)

Trail number and name

Bar colour indicates region*

Rating: Easy (1) Moderate (2) Difficult (3) Strenuous (4) Wilderness (W)

Tent icon indicates an overnight hike; compass icon indicates an unmarked trail (map and compass skills required)

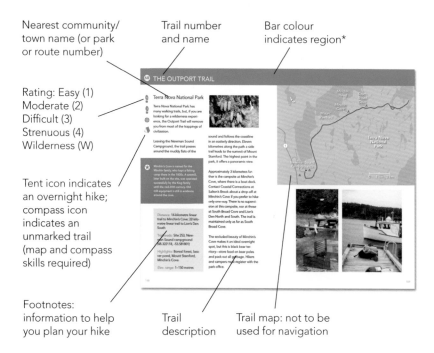

Footnotes: information to help you plan your hike

Trail description

Trail map: not to be used for navigation

*Bar colour key

Avalon Peninsula: trails of the Avalon other than the East Coast Trail

East Coast Trail: managed by the ECTA and found on the eastern coast of the Avalon Peninsula

Bonavista Peninsula: trails from Clarenville to the town of Bonavista

All around the Circle: Road to the Shore, Fogo Island, Change Islands, and Twillingate

Burin Peninsula: trails on the Burin Peninsula

Wilderness Trails: located in various locations in eastern Newfoundland

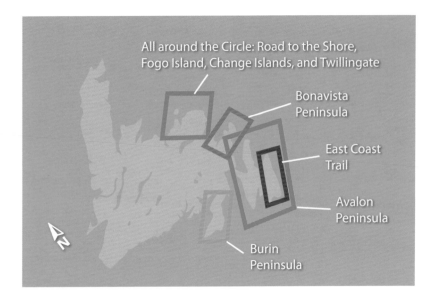

All around the Circle: Road to the Shore, Fogo Island, Change Islands, and Twillingate

Bonavista Peninsula

East Coast Trail

Avalon Peninsula

Burin Peninsula

More information about the page layout

The trails in the first five sections (Avalon Peninsula, the East Coast Trail, Bonavista Peninsula, Burin Peninsula and All around the Circle) are generally well-marked and -maintained; accommodations and other amenities for the visiting hiker are readily found nearby.

Wilderness Trails are more rugged trails that present certain challenges for hikers (see the introduction for Wilderness Trails, page 190, for details).

Trail Ratings: The trails in this book have been rated as Easy, Moderate, Difficult, or Strenuous. These terms and their descriptions have been borrowed with permission from the East Coast Trail Association because they are straightforward and easy to understand.

Easy: 2–7 kilometres long, typically with elevation changes less than 25 metres and good trail conditions.

Moderate: 4–11 kilometres long with elevation changes of usually less than 75 metres.

Difficult: 9–17 kilometres. Elevation changes up to 150 metres and more rugged trail conditions.

Strenuous: Usually longer distances with elevation changes of over 150 metres and rugged trail conditions.

Wilderness: Additionally, some trails are also indicated as wilderness trails; these are generally suitable for fit and experienced hikers. Hikes may require map and compass navigation and/or overnighting in a tent. Expect substantial elevation changes and very rugged, poorly maintained, or unmarked trails.

A second "boot" icon indicates a second trail or optional add-on hike or that the difficulty level falls between two levels. Please read the trail description for details.

Other icons:

The trail requires camping for one or more nights. If the tent icon is greyed-out, camping is optional—read the trail description for details. Tent sites indicated on the map are approximate locations, and subject to change. Amenities vary with the site.

The trail or route is unmarked or poorly marked; bring a map and compass and know how to use them. Do not rely only on a Global Positioning Device (GPD), such as a cell phone, or Global Positioning System (GPS).

Trail description: An overview of the hike, describing major junctions, lookout locations, and landmarks along the intended route. It also includes elevation changes, trail conditions, potential hazards, and other noteworthy information.

Maps: Maps provide the location of trailheads and a general indication of the trail route. The maps contain information gathered from the Toporama website of Natural Resources Canada and are subject to a degree of error. Topography lines are not shown; check the footnotes for expected elevation gain. Not all roads or landmarks are shown.

Disclaimer: The maps provided in this guide should not be used for navigation purposes. Detailed topographical maps are available for purchase from the provincial Department of Mines and Energy and would prove very useful for the Wilderness trails; they may be of use for other trails as well. The ECTA has produced a detailed set of maps of their trail.

Map legend

—— Road   ⋀ Campsite

⌇ Hiking trail   ⌶ Lighthouse

● Trailhead

Interesting information: Historical notes, natural feature highlights, geologic information, personal observations, and recommendations.

Footnotes

Distance: The hike length in kilometres (to the nearest half-kilometre) and trail type (loop, linear, or network).

Trailhead: Location of the trailhead(s); identifies parking areas and provides the decimal degrees of the main trailhead commonly used by GPS. GPS information is subject to a degree of error.

Highlights: What to watch for along the trail.

Elev. Range: Take the elevation range of the hikes into account when deciding whether to do the hike, and when.

Campsites: Any designated camping locations are listed.

A note about hiking times: Some hiking books give an estimated time for walking individual trails. We have not done so because walking paces depend on fitness levels, group size, trail conditions, and so on. Most people of average fitness can walk 4 to 5 kilometres in an hour on a smooth surface such as a road. That pace will slow down on a trail, however, because of the uneven surface and elevation changes. It is also important to allow for the limited daylight hours in late fall and early winter when earlier start times may be necessary.

Planning your hike

Newfoundland weather

Few topics in Newfoundland get more attention than the weather. We complain about our cool temperatures until the sun comes out; then we lament because it is so hot. Changeable conditions are the norm, so it is best to be prepared.

Clothing

Clothes don't make the hiker, but the right clothing can make the experience a more comfortable one. Experienced hikers will know what works best for them. Dressing in layers so that you can dress up or dress down according to the mercury on the thermometer is a good idea. A fleece vest or jacket is a valuable addition to the hiker's wardrobe, as is a windbreaker, preferably waterproof. A hat provides protection from sun and rain, and gloves are good to have at the bottom of the backpack for those days when it is cool or fog rolls in.

Footwear

Feet are a hiker's best friends, so it is important to be kind to them. A good pair of waterproof hiking boots makes for a happy hiker. If you are going to venture out on a trail only occasionally and in dry conditions, you can probably get by with a good pair of running or trail shoes.

Gaiters are useful in wet and muddy conditions and can also protect your legs in places where brush and branches have grown over the path.

Equipment

■ Backpacks are available in a variety of sizes and prices. Packs with a waist belt and a chest strap offer the best support for your back and will be more comfortable on longer hikes.

■ Hiking poles relieve stress on knees and hips, help with balance, and involve your upper body for a more complete exercise.

■ A water bottle should be your constant companion. It is important to keep hydrated.

■ Sunscreen and insect repellent are also important, for obvious reasons. It must be said, though, that on the coastal hikes we have rarely been bothered by mosquitoes or blackflies.

■ A pocketknife is a useful implement to carry at all times.

■ Binoculars can add enjoyment especially when observing birds, whales, or other wildlife.

■ It may seem trivial, but a gardening kneeling pad can prevent a wet bottom when sitting down for lunch or a snack.

■ First-aid kit, including Band-aids, calamine lotion, Aspirin, and a tension bandage.

Trail ethics

Respect the environment you are walking through and leave it as pristine as you found it. It goes without saying that no litter should be left behind, even if it is biodegradable. In the interests of preventing erosion, stay on the trail. In some areas, it is also dangerous to wander off the trail, especially as cliff edges may be unstable. For safety reasons it is better to use a small cooker rather than an open fire. Note: open fires may not be permitted in all locations or in all seasons.

Wildlife

Observing wildlife in their natural environment is one of the added benefits of hiking. Moose, caribou, foxes, coyotes, hares, whales, and many varieties of birds may all be encountered, although the larger land animals tend to be wary of human contact and keep their distance. Black bears also inhabit the island and encounters, though rare, are possible.

Common sense

- Tell someone where you are going and when you expect to return.
- Cellphones, while helpful, have restricted reception on some paths.
- Bring a water bottle; never underestimate the dangers of dehydration.
- Wildlife is just that: Treat it with due respect and use caution.

Some of the trails in this book are traditional footpaths that were once the only link between neighbouring communities. Many others originated as paths worn in by berry pickers, bird hunters, and woodcutters. Others have more recently been developed from scratch. It is due to the individuals, organizations, and communities responsible for preserving and developing these trails that we have access to a priceless wilderness experience. We owe them a huge debt of thanks.

Assumption of risk

Disclaimer: All outdoor activities, including hiking and walking, have inherent elements of risk. Most of the hikes in this book have marked and maintained trails and we strongly advise that you remain on these trails. Where trails are not as well-maintained, caution and common sense can usually get you through any situation.

This book serves as a guide only. It is the ultimate and sole responsibility of the user to determine which hikes are appropriate for his or her skill and fitness level. Readers and hikers also hold the ultimate and sole responsibility for being aware of changes and alert to any hazards that may have arisen since the writing of this book.

The Avalon Peninsula is the most densely populated area of Newfoundland and Labrador. The first permanent settlements in the region were established in the early 1600s; the area's rich cod fishery led to the steady growth of the region over the centuries.

Since the late 1990s, the offshore oil industry has spurred the rapid growth of towns and cities, particularly those in the northeast Avalon. This recent development does not mean, however, that one has to drive for hours to find the serenity and isolation of uninhabited wilderness. One of the attractions of the Avalon is the easy accessibility of walking trails that transport the hiker to places of startling natural beauty.

The terrain varies widely from one part of the Avalon to another. The treeless barrens and headlands of the southern shore or Cape St. Mary's seem a world apart from the thickly forested areas along the east coast. In some places, the land slopes gently to the sea; in others, sheer cliffs are a characteristic feature. The Labrador current brings changeable weather and encourages the subarctic vegetation of the Avalon. Hikers should be prepared for cool conditions no matter how congenial the weather when starting out; onshore winds can bring thick banks of fog on land and send the temperature plummeting.

The Avalon Peninsula trails display a variety of trail standards and infrastructure styles. Only the d'Iberville Trail takes a day to walk—and even that trail can be hiked in shorter sections. Butter Pot Hill is an inland trail; the others in this section are coastal trails.

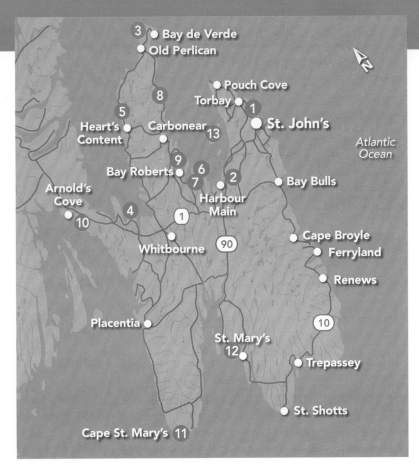

Trails of the Avalon Peninsula

1. Trails of Signal Hill / St. John's
2. Butter Pot Hill Trail / Butter Pot Provincial Park
3. Grates Cove Trails / Grates Cove
4. Sea View Trail / Norman's Cove
5. d'Iberville Trail / Heart's Content to Winterton
   and Hant's Harbour to New Chelsea
6. Brigus Lighthouse Trail / Brigus
7. Burnt Head Trail / Cupids
8. Blackhead to Western Bay / Blackhead (Conception Bay North)
9. Bay Roberts Shoreline Heritage Walk / Bay Roberts
10. Bordeaux Trail / Arnold's Cove
11. Bird Rock / Cape St. Mary's
12. St. Mary's to Gaskiers Trail / St. Mary's
13. Gregory Normore Walking Trail / Bell Island

2 St. John's

The trails of Signal Hill are part of the Grand Concourse system of trails around the city of St. John's. Trails on and around Signal Hill can be hiked separately or linked for a more challenging 5-kilometre hike. The loop trail described here is rated "moderate," although it does include a significant climb.

> ★ Cabot Tower was constructed atop Signal Hill in 1897 to celebrate Queen Victoria's Diamond Jubilee. That year also marked the 400th anniversary of Cabot's landfall in North America. Signal Hill is the site of the reception of the first transatlantic wireless signal by Gugliemo Marconi in 1901.

This trail is especially interesting for its geology. The Johnson Geo Centre on Signal Hill Road is a must-see either before or after the hike if you are interested in learning about the geological history of the area.

The Cuckold Cove Trail (also called the Burma Trail) begins at Georges Pond just above the Geo Centre. Park by Deadmans Pond, which is directly across the road from the Geo Centre. The trail passes by Georges Pond on the way to the Cuckold Cove Lookout just above Quidi Vidi village.

After taking in the view at Cuckold Cove Lookout, hike back up the trail for 250 metres, then turn left

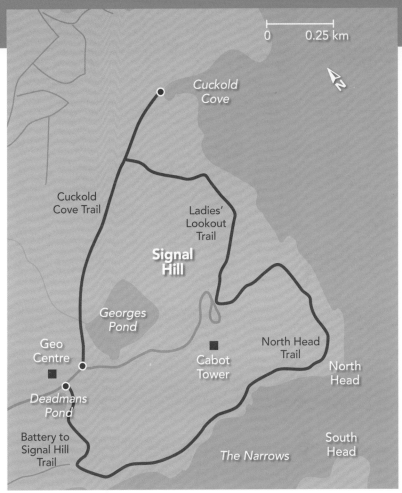

Trail maps are **not to be used for navigation.**

Distance: 5-kilometre loop

Trailhead: Georges Pond, Signal Hill Road (47.341916, -52.411553)

Highlights: Panoramic vistas, geological features, view of St. John's Harbour

Elev. Range: 12–140 metres

 Glacial erratics are debris transported by moving glaciers which, once the ice begins to melt, are deposited in no particular pattern in the landscape. These rocks vary in size; some on this trail are the size of a small car.

onto Ladies' Lookout Trail. A steep climb to the top on a series of wooden steps provides stunning views of St. John's to the west and the Atlantic Ocean to the east. Continue along the well-trodden trail to the Cabot Tower parking lot.

The North Head Trail, the next part of this loop, commences from the parking lot with a long stairway leading down into Ross's Valley, a glacial hanging valley created as the land rebounded (isostatic rebound) in the wake of a retreating ice cap some 10,000 years ago. Another obvious sign of glacial activity along this trail is the large glacial erratics or boulders. Less obvious to the eye but no less interesting are the stria or scratches on some of the massive flat stone surfaces on or beside the trail. These were created by

forward-moving glaciers pushing
sharp debris and making gouges
in the rock below the ice. The ice
was up to 3 kilometres thick during
the last ice age in this area of the
province. The direction of ice
movement can be determined by
these scratches. This trail passes
along the north shore of St. John's
Harbour, eventually arriving at the
Lower Battery.

Follow the road and turn right
onto Hipditch Hill. On the left look
for a staircase that goes up between two houses. Follow this trail

to Deadmans Pond and the parking lot. More information about
the Signal Hill trails is available at
the Parks Canada Interpretation
Centre on Signal Hill.

② Butter Pot Provincial Park

Butter Pot Provincial Park, 35 kilometres southwest of St. John's along the Trans-Canada Highway, has a number of walking trails, the most notable of which is the hike to the top of Butter Pot Hill.

 A *butter pot* describes a bare rounded hilltop, sometimes referred to as a tolt. This feature also exists in Renews and Northern Bay on the Avalon Peninsula, among other locations.

From the trailhead sign at campsite 67, follow the trail as it winds through boreal forest and past Pegwood Pond on its way to the base of the hill that gives this park its name. Watch for moose, birds, and signs of beaver activity along the way.

The summit of Butter Pot Hill is 300 metres above sea level. From it, the hiker has a bird's-eye view of the park and surrounding countryside.

The rounded pre-Cambrian rock that forms this hill is 600 million years old. Look for glacial erratics scattered over the bare hillside. This is a one-way path, so, after absorbing the view, enjoy the trail from the reverse angle on the way back.

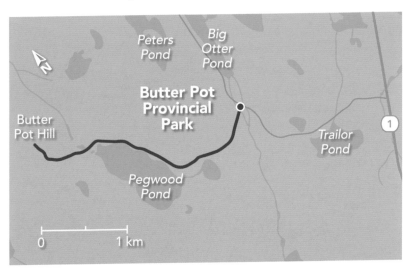

Trail maps are **not to be used for navigation.**

Distance: 3.3-kilometre linear trail (6.6-kilometre return)

Trailhead: Butter Pot Provincial Park, campsite 67 (47.233993, -53.034528)

Highlights: Mountaintop view, woodland path

Elev. Range: 155–300 metres

Grates Cove

Grates Cove, a community of about 200 people located at the northern tip of the Avalon Peninsula, has been inhabited by Europeans since the 17th century. Nearby Bay de Verde and Bacca-lieu Island, with its huge colony of seabirds, are two other places of interest in the area.

The Grates Cove area is devoid of trees but rich in rock, and residents put the available resources to good use. Grates Cove was designated as a National Historic Site in 1995 for its network of rock walls that enclose some 150 acres of land once used for grazing cattle, growing hay, and vegetable gardening.

Grates Cove boasts two short trails worth exploring. **Rock Walls Trail** begins on Back Road by the National Historic Site Memorial. This 2-kilometre loop trail is marked by blue arrows painted on stone, which unfortunately over time are becoming quite faded. The trail proceeds toward the coast past kilometres of stone walls and enclosures; the toil required to construct these walls

 Look for the three types of rock walls: *Thrown walls* are made of rocks cleared from fields and deposited in a row. *Piled walls* are made of some interlocking stone. *Stacked walls*, the most carefully constructed, reached heights of 1.5 metres.

Distance: See trail descriptions

Trailheads: Rock Walls Trail: Back Road (48.095900, -52.561900); Lookout Trail: Big Hill Road (48.093786, -52.564042)

Highlights: Rock walls, panoramic views, wildflowers

Elev. Range: Rock Walls Trail: minimal change; Lookout Trail, 79–115 metres

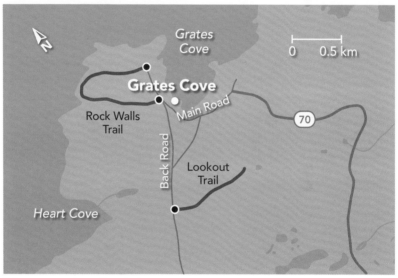

Trail maps are **not to be used for navigation.**

is awe-inspiring. The trail loops
back to end on Main Road several
hundred metres from the starting
point.

Lookout Trail begins on Big Hill
Road and climbs 1 kilometre to a
high bluff overlooking the town.
The trail consists of a boardwalk

that meanders its way to the top.
It is a steady climb and caution
should be taken on days with high
winds. The effort is rewarded by a
stunning view of Conception Bay,
Grates Cove, and the fields and
gardens delineated by the rock
walls below.

Norman's Cove

For a short hike with an extraordinary view, visit the Sea View Trail in Norman's Cove. Tucked into Chapel Arm at the bottom of Trinity Bay, this trail is a hidden gem.

 Wild roses are more than just attractive blossoms. Jams, syrup, jellies, and teas can be made from the ripened fleshy fruit or "hips" of the plant.

A sign on Hilltop Lane near the post office in Norman's Cove points the way to the trailhead and there is plenty of parking near the cemetery. Take the track to the left. Just before you reach another cemetery, the path descends toward the cove. Turn right at the shoreline, pass a little sandy beach, and then climb a small rise to the gazebo lookout. A boardwalk crosses a pleasant meadow; the trail next takes you through thick woods and, eventually, to a clearing. Across the clearing, a 130-step staircase leads to the summit on Chapel Head 63 metres above the bay.

The picnic table at the top is an ideal place to rest and take in the

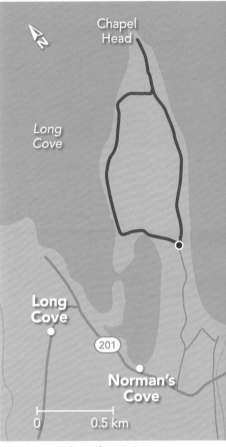

Trail maps are **not to be used for navigation.**

spectacular view of Chapel Arm, Long Cove, and the eastern shoreline of Trinity Bay. Continue along the trail as it gradually descends along the steeply angled sedimentary layers that make up the ridge of Chapel Head and brings you back to the trailhead.

Distance: 4-kilometre loop

Trailhead: Anglican Cemetery, Norman's Cove (47.340064, -53.393726)

Highlights: Views from Chapel Head, wild roses

Elev. Range: 0–63 metres

Heart's Content to Winterton / Hant's Harbour to New Chelsea

This trail system on the east side of Trinity Bay is named for Pierre Le Moyne d'Iberville, the French commander at Placentia who led a series of destructive raids on English fishing settlements in Newfoundland in 1696.

 Pierre Le Moyne d'Iberville, sent to Placentia from New France in 1696, began raiding coastal settlements at the Colony of Avalon (Ferryland). He proceeded north to St. John's, burning and looting along the way, and then moved to Conception and Trinity bays. A total of 36 settlements were destroyed, but by the following year they had all been reclaimed by England.

Most of this trail (from Heart's Content to Winterton) can be done as a long, single-day hike. Because the trail joins the road in several places, however, it may also be tackled as a series of shorter walks.

The trail starts at the brightly painted red and white lighthouse at Heart's Content. Parts of the trail consist of an elaborate boardwalk and wooden stairs which wind in and out of wooded areas. The first section, Heart's Content to New Perlican, ends on the south side of the community of New Perlican. Follow the road through New Perlican to find a sign to show where the trail continues. The trail follows the headland to Turk's Cove. At Turk's Cove, walk along the road again before rejoining the trail to Winterton.

Although the d'Iberville Trail occasionally travels inland, it does offer some coastal views. The lookout above Winterton is the highest point and, from it on fine days, you can see across Trinity Bay. The final section of the d'Iberville Trail begins in Hant's Harbour and ends in the charming community of New Chelsea. This segment takes only an hour to walk but it climbs to 80 metres before descending into New Chelsea.

Even though the trail is segmented by Route 80, it is not difficult to locate; signs give clear directions to the trailheads and parking areas.

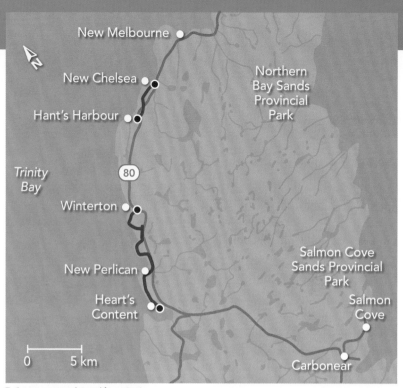

New Melbourne

New Chelsea

Hant's Harbour

Trinity Bay

80

Winterton

New Perlican

Heart's Content

Northern Bay Sands Provincial Park

Salmon Cove Sands Provincial Park

Salmon Cove

Carbonear

0   5 km

Trail maps are **not to be used for navigation.**

Distance: 20-kilometre linear trail

Trailheads: Heart's Content Lighthouse (47.543175, -53.213002); Winterton (47.571616, -53.195041); Hant's Harbour (48.005097, 53.153002); New Chelsea (48.013916, -53.131324)

Highlights: Ocean views

Elev. Range: 0–100 metres

2 Brigus

The lighthouse at Northern Head, the destination of this trail, seems deceptively close as you start the hike. The terrain and meandering nature of the trail makes this a bigger challenge than meets the eye.

The trailhead for this 5-kilometre hike is on Battery Road on the north side of Brigus. The hike gets under way with a fairly steep climb to the top of the ridge. Take a brief rest at the top and enjoy the view back to the historic town of Brigus. The town is renowned for its architecture, rock walls, and the annual Blueberry Festival that attracts thousands of people each August.

From the ridge, the trail descends into a valley and Brigus is lost to view. The path is not flagged, but keep in mind that the destination is the lighthouse and, if you are in doubt, stick to the high ground and keep the ocean on your right. Finding the way is not difficult.

Allow about one and a half hours to reach the automated lighthouse. Don't be surprised if you see a small herd of goats browsing in the area. Enjoy the views from this headland before making the return journey.

Near the trailhead is Kent Cottage, a house that was occupied during the early years of World War I by American artist Rockwell Kent. He was expelled from Newfoundland on suspicion of being a German spy, although it was later recognized that the charges were bogus. Kent paid a return visit to Newfoundland at the invitation of Premier Joseph Smallwood in 1968.

Distance: 2.5-kilometre linear trail (5-kilometre return)

Trailhead: Battery Road, Brigus (47.322572, -53.122413)

Highlights: Dramatic terrain, lighthouse

Elev. Range: 12–102 metres

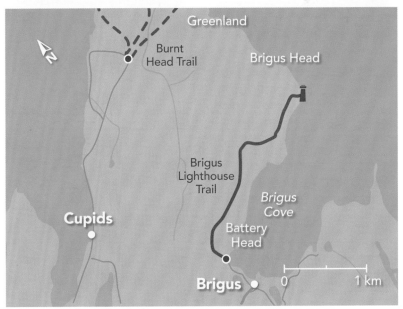

Trail maps are **not to be used for navigation.**

Cupids

This trail network explores the Burnt Head-Greenland area near Cupids, Conception Bay. Cupid's Haven B&B and Tea Room at the end of Bishop's Lane is the starting point for this hike, which leads to the northeast through woods before emerging onto an open headland with meadows and beaches.

Distance:
5-kilometre trail network

Trailhead: Cupid's Haven B&B
(47.335025, -53.115546)

Highlights: Sea arch
(47.341905, -53.11315)

Elev. Range: 0–60 metres

At the first fork in the trail, veer to the right in the direction of Greenland. The trail passes through a cozy sheltered picnic area and over a stream on the way to Morgan's Cove then to a viewing platform at Noder Cove. The sloping rock formations on the beach below are impressive. The trail proceeds up Windy Hill, arriving at The Arch. Take care around the edges of the cliff while taking pictures.

The trail continues up the hill to Deep Gulch and then returns to the starting point at the St. Augustine Anglican Cemetery directly across from the B&B.

★ Cupids was founded by John Guy in 1610, making it the second oldest English colony in North America after Jamestown, Virginia. Originally called Cuper's Cove, the colony was abandoned in 1700. Since the 1990s, archaeologists have uncovered thousands of artifacts and several building foundations. Many of these discoveries are on display at the Cupids Legacy Centre, which opened in 2010.

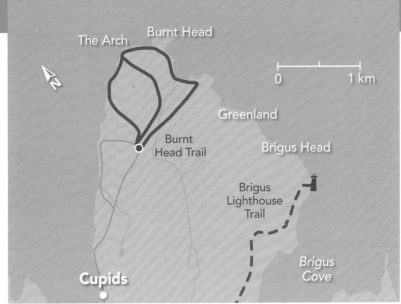

The Arch Burnt Head

Greenland

Brigus Head

Burnt Head Trail

Brigus Lighthouse Trail

Brigus Cove

Cupids

0   1 km

Trail maps are **not to be used** for navigation.

Blackhead

On the west side of Conception Bay, the small community of Blackhead marks the start of a gentle hike that terminates about 7 kilometres to the north in Western Bay. Despite a lack of signs, the path is easy to follow as a well-used track parallels the coastline at least as far as Bradley's Cove.

Turn off Route 70 onto Gander Road in Blackhead. The hike begins where the cart track cuts through woods and blueberry

Wild berries are a common sight on many of the hiking trails in Newfoundland. The colourful northern wild raisin found here is edible but not as popular or tasty as the blueberry or partridgeberry.

patches toward the shoreline. Follow the track as it passes a tiny overgrown graveyard; then the trees and bushes give way to a rugged coastline on the right and open meadows on the left.

The track brings you into the little settlement of Adam's Cove. Skirt to the left of the last house and keep heading north. Until Adam's Cove, the track is nearly level but high bare hills in the distance indicate some climbing lies ahead. At the top of the first hill enjoy the view. On clear days you can see across Conception Bay.

Below the hill is a large grassy valley. Bradley's Cove was once a thriving community but all that remains, except for a small flock of sheep, is a root cellar. The cellar, built by expert stonemasons, looks like a turf-covered igloo. The entrance to the cellar is accessible, but enter at your own risk. A small rocky beach nearby is an excellent place to stop and have lunch.

From Bradley's Cove, you have two options: stick with the cart track for the shortcut into West-

Trail maps are **not to be used for navigation.**

ern Bay, or keep to the right and continue out to the point, where there is an automated light in place of a lighthouse. This is a good place for whale and seabird spotting—we have seen gannets plunging from great heights into the sea. A well-used path leads to a parking area at the end of River Road in Western Bay.

Distance:
5- or 7-kilometre linear trail

Trailheads: Gander Road, Blackhead (47.510523, -53.053527); River Road, Western Bay (47.530133, -53.041344)

Highlights: Ocean views, root cellar

Elev. Range: Minimal change

Bay Roberts

The trailhead for this walk is situated just off Water Street in Bay Roberts East. A large sign directs hikers to a parking area at the start of the trail.

This is an 8-kilometre loop trail that combines history, culture, and scenery. A well-developed path leads hikers past signs which identify families who once dried fish and tended gardens along this shore. Several retaining walls, foundations, and root cellars have been restored by the Heritage Society; these structures prove that the local residents were also skilled stonemasons.

The path briefly joins a narrow paved road and then veers off in the direction of French's Cove. French's Cove was settled in the 17th century and destroyed twice by French raiders, in 1696 and 1705. A large photograph mounted on an interpretive panel in French's Cove shows what the community looked like before resettlement.

The landscape becomes more dramatic as the trail leads toward Juggler's Cove, with deep coves and high craggy cliffs providing views across Conception Bay. At the end of the peninsula lie Mad Rocks, which, as the name implies, can turn the shoreline into a mad fury in heavy seas.

From this point you can follow the road back to the trailhead, or, in the vicinity of Mad Rocks Café, you can loop back across the peninsula to French's Cove and return to the trailhead along the path.

Mad Rocks

French's Cove

Spaniard's Bay

Port de Grave

Bay Roberts

70

0   1 km

Trail maps are not to be used for navigation.

Distance:
8-kilometre loop

Trailhead: Water Street,
Bay Roberts East
(47.361598, -53.135439)

Highlights: Root cellars,
stone walls, seascapes

Elev. Range:
3–45 metres

Arnold's Cove

Early French settlers called this area Bordeaux after their homeland in France. In the 1800s, James Adams and his family farmed the land here for over a century. A plaque has been mounted in the vicinity of the Adams family homestead.

Signs in Arnold's Cove point to the trailhead at the end of Monkstown Road, where there is ample parking. Across the bay, Merasheen Island is visible in the distance. The largest island in Placentia Bay, Merasheen Island was resettled in the 1960s.

The first part of the trail follows the shoreline, crossing beaches and grassy headlands. The Horse Meadows, Lou Point, Labours Cove, and Wild Cove are all places of interest along the way. Some old house foundations can still be seen.

This headland has long been considered an attractive place to live. Archaeologists have uncovered evidence that shows Dorset Eskimos, Beothuk Indians, and Basque fishers all spent time there.

On the side of the main road into Arnold's Cove is the Big Pond Bird Sanctuary. This is a popular pit stop for many migratory birds, including Canada geese, pie ducks, mallards, ruddy turnstones, and sandpipers. Ospreys and bald eagles may also be seen.

The trail eventually crosses over the headland to a meadow which provides a different view of the bay and, in the distance, the trans-shipment oil facility at Whiffen Head. This is an excellent spot to relax or stop for lunch.

Allow half a day for this hike and take time for some beachcombing and exploring.

Distance: 10-kilometre loop

Trailhead: Monkstown Rd., Arnold's Cove (47.454981, -53.592369)

Highlights: Beaches, views of the bay

Elev. Range: 0–25 metres

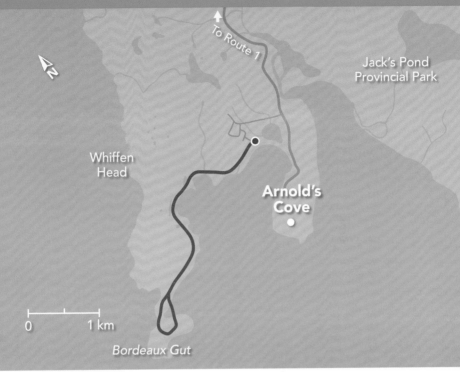

Jack's Pond
Provincial Park

To Route 1

Whiffen
Head

**Arnold's
Cove**

0   1 km

Bordeaux Gut

Trail maps are **not to be used for navigation.**

Wild Cove

Cape St. Mary's

The walk to Bird Rock at Cape St. Mary's is a short stroll rather than a hike, but the destination is so iconic it is impossible to ignore. Anyone who has visited this site can't help but be awed by the immense open headland at the Cape … and then there are the birds.

The Cape St. Mary's Ecological Reserve is home to common murres, black-legged kittiwakes, razorbills, and 24,000 northern gannets. The northern gannets, graceful seabirds with a wingspan of 2 metres, hatch their young on a 100-metre-high sea stack a few metres from the cliff edge. Bird Rock is the third largest, and the most accessible, nesting site for northern gannets in North America. It is endlessly fascinating to watch the birds swoop and soar as they dive for fish to feed their young.

Spring and early summer is the best time to observe the hatchlings, but foggy conditions are common at those times of the year. Late summer and early autumn usually bring warmer weather and clear skies.

Visit the interesting displays at the Interpretation Centre. The Centre also hosts a summer concert series that features traditional storytellers and musicians. Accommodations are available in nearby St. Brides.

 Gannets occupy the same nest year after year. In late spring, the female lays a single egg which both parents take turns incubating until it hatches in early July. The young chick is fully feathered by September and, soon afterwards, makes its first awkward attempts at flight. Then it is on its own and must learn how to feed itself once its body fat has been used up.

Distance: 1-kilometre linear trail (2-kilometre return)

Trailhead: Cape St. Mary's Interpretation Centre (46.492310, -54.113192)

Highlights: Cliffs, headland, birds

Elev. Range: Minimal

To Route 100

Brierly
Cove

Golden
Bay

Cape
St. Mary's

Bird
Rock

0   1 km

Trail maps are **not to be used for** navigation.

② St. Mary's

This route along the eastern shore of St. Mary's Bay, part ATV track and part traditional footpath, is used primarily by berry pickers. Although it is not a developed trail, and there are no signs, the trail is not difficult to locate or follow.

You can park near the community wharf in Gaskiers and at the trailhead in St. Mary's; or, if you prefer a shorter hike, park at the beach in Gulch.

In St. Mary's, turn off Route 90 onto Dillon's Lane and then take Battery Road a short distance to the trailhead at the Battery. Join the Back Road and follow it in a southeasterly direction until you reach a narrow footpath veering off to the right.

The footpath hugs the rugged shoreline, passing over blueberry barrens and country rich in wildflowers and grasses. It is easy walking, with little change in elevation. The depth of the peat just below the surface becomes evident as the path nears the automated light near Gulch. A picnic table near the light is a good place to stop for lunch if you have timed your arrival right.

Continue south over the meadow to the kilometre-long stony beach that separates Point La Haye Pond from the ocean. Crossing the beach is quite a slog and can be avoided by leaving a car at Gulch rather than Gaskiers. Otherwise, cross the beach, which forms a large freshwater barachois to the northeast, and follow the road through Point La Haye and Gaskiers to the community wharf.

Distance: 8-kilometre linear trail

Trailhead: The Battery, St. Mary's (46.551855, -53.345341); community wharf in Gaskiers (46.574444, -53.364603)

Highlights: Coastline, barachois, beaches, barrens

Elev. Range: 5–35 metres

St. Mary's

St. Mary's
Bay

Gulch

Gaskiers
Bay

Gaskiers

90

0   1 km

Trail maps are **not to be used for navigation.**

Bell Island

The Gregory Normore Walking Trail, named for the first settler on Bell Island (1740), circumnavigates most of Bell Island. It is 24 kilometres in total but can be walked in shorter segments.

The obvious place to start is from Beach Hill, the first hill you meet after leaving the ferry dock. You'll find this trailhead on your right side, partway up the hill. Parking is available at the viewing platform on the left side of the road.

Follow an ATV track up the hill until you arrive at an old graveyard that contains the headstone of Gregory Normore. At this point, the ATV track veers to the left but **hikers should keep right**, closer to the coast, and follow the trail through the trees.

Once you have passed through the small forest, you'll catch a spectacular view across the tickle to Portugal Cove and Bauline. The cliffs on this side of the island are high and steep and offer the opportunity to photograph the geology of the island. As the trees thin, the path enters the open meadowland that characterizes much of this trail as it continues on north and westward around the island.

Distance: 24-kilometre linear trail (Beach Hill to lighthouse: 5-kilometre linear trail)

Trailhead: Beach Hill (47.375276, -52.552537); Belle Road (47.355798, -53.004263)

Highlights: Steep cliffs, views of Conception Bay, The Bell

Elev. Range: 23–102 metres

The lighthouse and the Keeper's Café are approximately 5 kilometres from the trailhead and make a fitting place to stop if you are looking for a shorter hike. Beyond the lighthouse look for places named Freshwater Cove, #2 Cove, Grebe's Nest, Ochre Pit Cove, and The Bell. From Belle Road to Lance Cove there is no trail. The path resumes just to the east of Lance Cove Beach and continues on to the trail-head at Beach Hill.

This path is rated difficult, due to its length only.

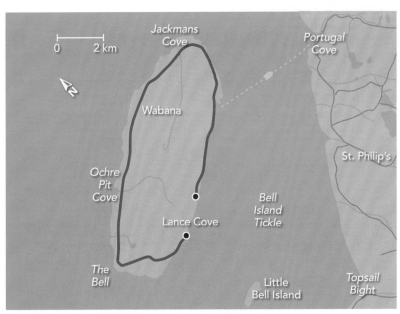

Trail maps are **not to be used for navigation.**

THE EAST COAST TRAIL

To many, hiking in Newfoundland means hiking the East Coast Trail. This series of coastal paths stretching from Portugal Cove north to Cape St. Francis and then down the east coast of the Avalon Peninsula to St. John's and south to Cappahayden constitute a remarkable hiking experience.

As of 2016, over 300 kilometres of trail have been developed. Plans are in place to further extend the trail network along the shoreline of Conception Bay to Topsail Beach. The trail links many communities, providing an accessible wilderness experience for the hiker.

Trail infrastructure has been built with an eye to interfering as little as possible with the natural environment. Numerous bridges have been built to facilitate stream crossings, including the impressive suspension bridge at La Manche.

But it is the coastal scenery, not the infrastructure, that makes this trail outstanding. Path lengths vary as does the degree of difficulty, but the one constant is the trail's proximity to the ocean and the coastline, beaches, coves, and cliffs.

The ECTA was founded in 1994 with the goal of developing a coastal trail for the use of residents and visitors. It has created access to some of the most beautiful coastline anywhere in the world. To walk the East Coast Trail is to be immersed in not only the geography but also the culture and history of the east coast of this province.

New members are invited to join this volunteer-run association. More information about the trail is available at www.eastcoasttrail.ca.

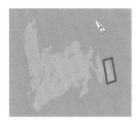

The East Coast Trail

14. Picco's Ridge Path / Portugal Cove-Bauline
15. White Horse Path / Bauline to Cape St. Francis
16. Biscan Cove Path / Cape St. Francis to Pouch Cove
17. Stiles Cove Path / Pouch Cove to Flatrock
18. Father Troy's Trail / Flatrock to Torbay
19. Silver Mine Head Path / Torbay to Middle Cove
20. Cobbler Path / Outer Cove to Logy Bay
21. Sugarloaf Path / Logy Bay to St. John's
22. Deadmans Bay Path / St. John's to Blackhead
23. Blackhead Path / Blackhead to Cape Spear
24. Cape Spear Path / Cape Spear to Maddox Cove
25. Motion Path / Petty Harbour to Goulds
26. Spout Path / Goulds to Bay Bulls
27. Mickeleens Path / Bay Bulls to Witless Bay
28. Beaches Path / Witless Bay to Mobile
29. Tinkers Point Path / Mobile to Tors Cove
30. La Manche Village Path / Bauline East to La Manche
31. Flamber Head Path / La Manche to Brigus South
32. Brigus Head Path / Brigus South to Admiral's Cove
33. Cape Broyle Head Path / Cape Broyle to Calvert
34. Caplin Bay Path / Calvert to Ferryland
35. Sounding Hills Path / Ferryland to Aquaforte
36. Mudder Wet Path / Aquaforte to South West River
37. Spurwink Island Path / South West River to Port Kirwan
38. Bear Cove Point Path / Kingman's Cove to Renews
39. Island Meadow Path / Renews to Cappahayden

Cape
St. Francis
16 Pouch Cove
15
17
Flatrock
Bauline
18
19 20
Torbay
14
21
St. John's
22 23
24
25

Conception
Bay

Bell
Island
Portugal Cove-
St. Philip's

10

1

26

Bay Bulls
27

Witless Bay

28

29

30

31

32

Cape Broyle
33

Avalon
Peninsula
34
35 Ferryland

36 37

Fermeuse
38

Renews

39

Cappahayden

Atlantic
Ocean

Portugal Cove to Bauline

This path has been used for many years, but changes in 2015 have made it a much-improved trail. New trailheads have been established at both ends, and the northern half of the route has been redirected so that it continues along the top of Picco's Ridge.

In Portugal Cove, take Loop Drive opposite the United Church, and turn down Harding's Hill to North Point Road, which leads to the new trailhead. In Bauline, use the parking lot at the end of Brook Path, where signs direct you to the trailhead.

Starting on the Portugal Cove side, the path leaves the ferry terminal behind as it climbs fairly steeply up newly built stairs to the top of the ridge and soon passes the Blast Hole Ponds. A farther 3 kilometres to the north is Brocks Head Pond, which empties dramatically over the cliff into Conception Bay far below. To the west, rising out of the waters of the bay, is Bell Island.

At Ocean Pond, the path turns briefly westward and then continues to the north along the top of the ridge all the way to Bauline (those familiar with the previous route will remember the trail travelled inland after Ocean Pond).

This is rugged country and at the time of publication the path had not been "hardened." Although there is little infrastructure along the trail, it is well marked and hikers should have no problem keeping on the correct route. Expect a wilderness experience with outstanding views both inland and seaward.

Distance: 14.5-kilometre linear trail

Trailhead: North Point Road, Portugal Cove (47.374663, -52.512882); Brook Path, Bauline (47.431696, -52.495649)

Highlights: Ponds, rivers, views of the ocean and Bell Island

Elev. Range: 14–242 metres

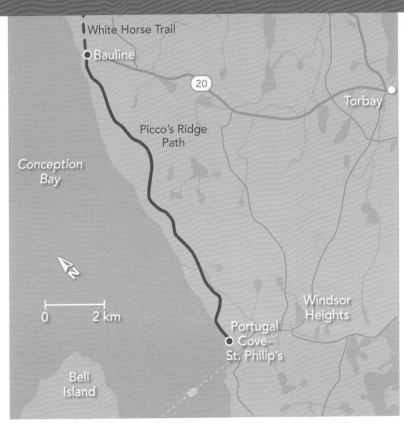

White Horse Trail

○ Bauline

20

Torbay

Picco's Ridge
Path

*Conception
Bay*

N

0   2 km

Windsor
Heights

Portugal
○ Cove-
St. Philip's

Bell
Island

Trail maps are **not to be used for navigation.**

WHITE HORSE PATH

Bauline to Cape St. Francis

This new hiking trail (as of 2015) incorporates the old Cripple Cove Path from Cape St. Francis and extends all the way to the town of Bauline on the eastern shore of Conception Bay. No trail infrastructure such as boardwalks or wooden stairs have been added as of 2015. Hikers should expect wilderness conditions, as well as a challenge: this trail features considerable elevation changes.

The trailhead in Bauline is at the end of Seaview Lane. Parking is available at Brook Path. On the northern end, the trailhead is near the automated light at Cape St. Francis—watch for the familiar East Coast Trail signs.

Distance: 17.5-kilometre linear trail

Trailhead: Cape St. Francis (47.48275, -52.47120); Bauline, Seaview Lane (47.43169, -52.49564)

Highlights: Rugged wilderness, ocean views, berries

Elev. Range: 14–240 metres

The trail from Cape St. Francis into Cripple Cove features steep climbs but the most challenging is yet to come. After Cripple Cove the path ascends to the top of the ridge 200 metres above sea level. Views along this rugged path are nothing short of spectacular.

At Little Herring Cove Pond (47.44274, -52.49153), an access path leads to Marine Park on Pouch Cove Line. This access path is in very rough condition. The main path continues south toward Bauline.

Before the path descends to the southern trailhead, a popular side trail goes to the peak of Big Hill, which towers 260 metres above the town and bay.

Biscan Cove
Path

Stiles Cove
Path

Pouch
Cove

Shoe
Cove

20

White Horse
Path

Marine
Park

Lower
Herring
Cove

Bauline

0   2 km

Picco's Ridge
Path

21

Trail maps are **not to be used for navigation.**

Cape St. Francis to Pouch Cove

Most sections of the East Coast Trail are linear trails, but loop hikes can sometimes be made by following a road back to the starting point. This is such a trail. The return road is a rough gravel road; if you choose to have a vehicle waiting at the northern end of the trail, make sure it has good clearance.

The southern trailhead is at the end of the pavement in Pouch Cove by the sign that commemorates the event of the sinking of the *Waterwitch*. Parking for hikers' vehicles is available at the ballpark about 250 metres south of the Waterwitch trailhead.

This is a fairly hilly hike with several small brooks and streams to cross. The first part of the trail leads hikers through the woods, emerging after five minutes near Horrid Gulch. It then winds to the top of Big Bald Head, which provides a view of Pouch Cove and the coastline to the south. Black and white wooden posts mark the trail on the exposed rocky outcrops.

A side path at Freshwater leads to the shoreline and a 3-metre waterfall, an ideal place to stop. The trail climbs once more to a high ridge before descending and coming out to the gravel road just south of Cape St. Francis lighthouse.

In 1875 the schooner *Waterwitch* was heading to her home port in Cupids when she ran aground in Horrid Gulch at Pouch Cove. Men from the community responded and lowered Alfred Moores over the cliff with a "hempen rope." A letter written by Reverend Reginald Johnson of Pouch Cove to *The Times* explained that "there were twenty-five souls on board out of which [they] saved only thirteen." For his heroic efforts, Moores was awarded a medal by the Humane Society of Liverpool.

Distance: 7.3-kilometre linear trail (plus 4 kilometres on the road to complete the loop)

Trailheads: Pouch Cove (47.463184, -52.455216); Cape St. Francis (47.475704, -52.472425)

Highlights: View from Big Bald Head, Freshwater

Elev. Range: 20–123 metres

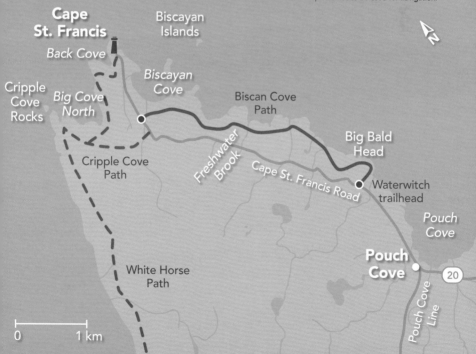

Trail maps are **not** to be used for navigation.

Cape St. Francis

Back Cove

Biscayan Islands

Biscayan Cove

Cripple Cove Rocks

Big Cove North

Biscan Cove Path

Cripple Cove Path

Freshwater Brook

Cape St. Francis Road

Big Bald Head

Waterwitch trailhead

Pouch Cove

White Horse Path

Pouch Cove

Pouch Cove Line

20

0   1 km

Pouch Cove to Flatrock

 If you're looking for a 15-kilometre day hike, Stiles Cove Path from Flatrock to Pouch Cove is as good as it gets. Rivers, waterfalls, bridges, coves, and cliffs—this trail has it all.

At Stiles Cove you will see a sobering reminder that it is dangerous to hike by the ocean. A cross and plaque memorialize a young couple who were swept off the rocks by a wave in 1993.

In Flatrock the path begins at the end of Hickey's Lane with parking at St. Michael's Church. The trail crosses over the dramatic Big River by way of a beautiful arched bridge. Steps have been cut in the stone by the trail builders for easier footholds. The trail continues through boreal forest, climbing gradually toward the top of the massive red sandstone cliff of Red Head.

From Red Head, follow the trail markers 4 kilometres north to Stiles Cove. Here Half Moon Brook tumbles over the cliff to a rocky beach below. Walk to the lookout point on the other side of the little bay and note how the water from the Half Moon Brook disappears into the beach rocks below rather than making a path to the ocean. Continuing north, the meadow at Small Point is an ideal spot to stop for lunch; it is approximately halfway to Pouch Cove.

Leaving Small Point, the trail eventually reaches its highest elevation of just over 100 metres before descending to sea level at Shoe Cove, where a bridge crosses Shoe Cove Brook. On the beach a rocky bar attempts to block the river on its unstoppable journey to the sea.

Several kilometres to the north, the trail leaves the woods, passes along the shoreline, and finally arrives at Pouch Cove post office and the northern trailhead.

This trail can be done in short segments as there are access trails to the main path at Shoe Cove, Satellite Road, and Red Head.

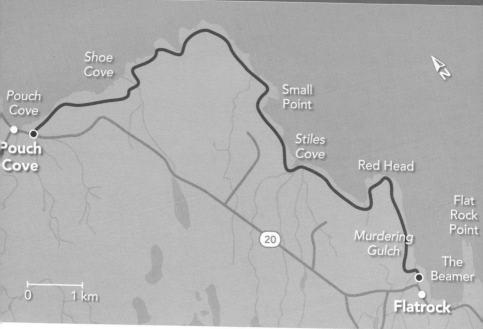

Pouch
Cove

Shoe
Cove

Pouch
Cove

Pouch
Cove

Small
Point

Stiles
Cove

Red Head

Flat
Rock
Point

Murdering
Gulch

The
Beamer

Flatrock

20

0   1 km

Trail maps are **not to be used** for navigation.

Distance: 15-kilometre linear trail

Trailheads: Pouch Cove (park at St. Agnes' Church, 47.455170, -52.455377); Flatrock (park at St. Michael's Church, 47.422609, -52.422890)

Highlights: Big River, Stiles Cove, Small Point, Shoe Cove

Elev. Range: 0–103 metres

18 FATHER TROY'S TRAIL

2 Flatrock to Torbay

This historic trail links the towns of Torbay and Flatrock. Father Troy's Trail begins at the end of Spray Lane. After crossing the beach, you will climb to the hillside meadows on the north side of the harbour.

The trail passes through Tapper's Cove and then begins a gradual ascent and soon enters thick woods. Church Cove is one of the highlights of this path ... literally. At 120 metres above sea level it provides a spectacular view of the cliff face, which is usually alive with shrieking gulls and kittiwakes.

From Church Cove, the trail follows along the top of the ridge for nearly 2 kilometres before descending to a sharp point of land that juts out into the Atlantic, known locally as the Beamer. The trail approaches the top of the Beamer, turns back, and ends at the parking area near the wharf and breakwater at Flatrock.

> ★ The trail is named for Father Edward Troy, who built the first Catholic Church in Torbay in the early 1830s. He was banished to Merasheen Island for several years for offending church leaders and politicians, but returned to Torbay in 1848 and was the parish priest there until his death in 1872.

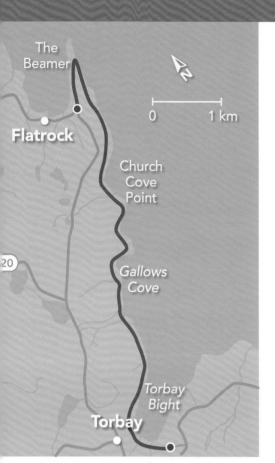

Trail maps are **not to be used for navigation.**

Distance:
8.7-kilometre linear trail

Trailhead: End of Spray Lane in Torbay (47.393309, -52.433443); breakwater in Flatrock (47.420230, -52.420818)

Highlights: Torbay, Church Cove, Beamer

Elev. Range: 2–120 metres

1 Torbay to Middle Cove

This is a short path but the difficulty in crossing Motion River, which is 2 kilometres from Middle Cove Beach, usually forces hikers to turn back at that point.

Begin at the north end of Middle Cove Beach, one of the most popular destinations on the northeast Avalon due to its beauty and proximity to the capital city of St. John's (and, in early summer, for

the caplin that roll on its shores during spawning season). Leaving the beach the trail climbs gradually and enters the woods.

After 1 kilometre the path emerges from the woods onto a meadow and leads to Motion, so named because of the mesmerizing swirl of currents and waves just offshore. It is not uncommon to see waves exploding against the cliffs and sending foam and spray high into the air.

Motion River, also known as North Pond Brook, can be crossed if water levels are low, but slippery rocks make this an uncertain venture. If you are successful in crossing the river, the path passes near the cliffs of Motion Head and ends 400 metres later at Motion Drive in Torbay.

 "Motion" is commonly used in association with Newfoundland coastal waters. The *Dictionary of Newfoundland English* defines it as "a stretch of water, the turbulent movement of which is caused by the meeting of heavy cross-currents."

Distance:
2.4-kilometre linear trail

Trailheads: Middle Cove Beach (47.390141, -52.414712); Motion Drive, Torbay (47.394414, -52.423339)

Highlights: Middle Cove Beach, Motion

Elev. Range: 0–23 metres

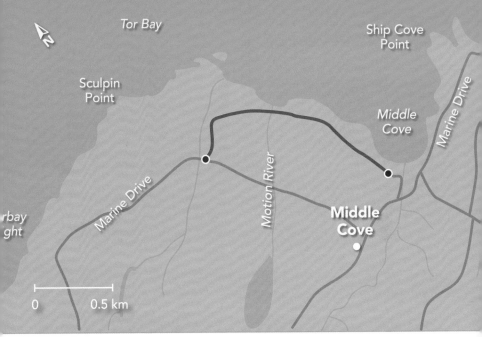

Tor Bay

Ship Cove Point

Sculpin Point

Middle Cove

Marine Drive

Marine Drive

Motion River

rbay ght

Middle Cove

0   0.5 km

Trail maps are **not to be used for navigation.**

Outer Cove to Logy Bay

Cobbler Path takes its name from the brook that crosses the trail midway through the hike. It is a short but fairly strenuous hike with two major hills to negotiate, but the views reward the effort. There is parking at both the Doran's Lane and Red Cliff Road trailheads.

At the end of Doran's Lane, a well-developed trail disappears into the woods and, in fewer than 10 minutes, opens out onto a magnificent ocean vista. A side trail to Klondyke Gulch on the left provides a view of Outer Cove and descends nearly to the ocean. The main trail goes right and up a high hill called Torbay Southern Head; pause to appreciate the stunning view back from the high point onto Klondyke Gulch.

 Many of the structures on Red Cliff were built in the early 1950s when the site became part of the Pinetree Line which extended across Canada. It was established during the height of the Cold War as part of a North American radar defence system. Nearly 250 people worked there before it was abandoned in 1961.

The trail then skirts the cliff edge 130 metres above the water, offering hikers views to the south, before it veers into the woods for the descent into Shooting Point Cove and Cobbler Brook. The path, having nearly arrived at sea level, turns upward once again in the direction of Red Cliff.

The top of Red Cliff is peppered with many abandoned concrete structures, some of which date to World War II when gun batteries were installed to defend against possible enemy attacks. Take time to enjoy the heart-stopping view over the cliff edge to the ocean some 150 metres below. From Red Cliff, you can keep to the trail that goes along the clifftop or take the road. You will soon come to a gravel lane that leads back out to Red Cliff Road.

Distance:
8-kilometre linear trail

Trailheads: Doran's Lane, Outer Cove (47.392152, -52.402483); Red Cliff Road, Logy Bay (47.381796, -52.401325)

Highlights: Klondyke Gulch, Red Cliff

Elev. Range: 3–150 metres

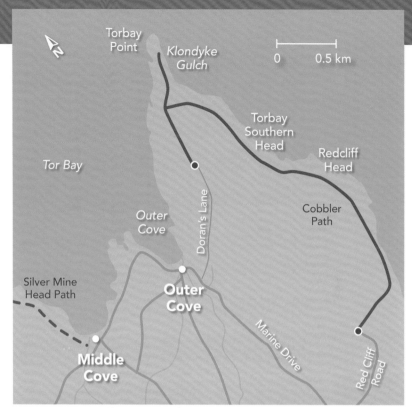

Torbay Point

Klondyke Gulch

Torbay Southern Head

Redcliff Head

Tor Bay

Doran's Lane

Outer Cove

Cobbler Path

Silver Mine Head Path

Outer Cove

Marine Drive

Middle Cove

Red Cliff Road

0   0.5 km

Trail maps are **not to be used for navigation.**

Logy Bay to St. John's

This linear path has designated parking near the Ocean Sciences Centre in Logy Bay and near two fluid storage tanks by the northern entrance to Quidi Vidi village.

Beginning in Quidi Vidi, the path provides various views of the village and the "gut," as the little harbour

 The dummy gun bunker on this path is typical of several that can be seen along the East Coast Trail. They were constructed during the war in response to the threat from German U-boats. The fake guns are long gone but the stone constructions, though in disrepair, are still visible.

Sugar-loaf: in designation of a prominent hill resembling in its shape a cone of refined sugar (Dictionary of Newfoundland English).

Distance:
9-kilometre linear trail

Trailheads: Quidi Vidi (unpaved road near end of lake, 47.345890, -52.403829); Logy Bay (next to Ocean Sciences Centre, 47.372550, -52.394749)

Highlights: Quidi Vidi, Bawdens Highlands, Sugarloaf Head

Elev. Range: 0–140 metres

is called. During the climb to the summit of Bawdens Highlands, hikers should watch for mountain bikers—mountain bike trails crisscross the area. Signs denote which paths are specifically designated for each activity.

Take a breather at the top and enjoy the panoramic view. Two kilometres farther along the trail, you will descend to near sea level by the pumphouse at Pump House Road; walk up a gravel road for a short distance, and then enter the woods. After passing rock formations at the Skerries, you cross the substantial John Howards footbridge, skirt Robin Hood Bay landfill, and begin the long ascent to the top of Sugarloaf Head with its panoramic ocean views. Watch for bald eagles and fox holes along the route.

Look for the old World War II dummy gun bunker that was meant to convince enemy U-boat captains that Newfoundland defences were more robust than they actually were.

Trail maps are **not to be used for navigation.**

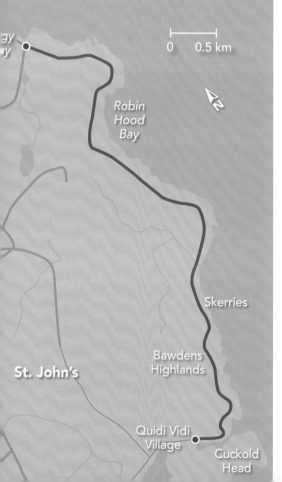

St. John's

Robin
Hood
Bay

Skerries

Bawdens
Highlands

Quidi Vidi
Village

Cuckold
Head

gy
y

0   0.5 km

St. John's to Blackhead

This path links the Fort Amherst lighthouse on the south side of St. John's Harbour at the Narrows with the tiny community of Blackhead situated just off Cape Spear Road.

Beginning near the Fort Amherst lighthouse, the path climbs steeply to a height of land level with Cabot Tower just across the Narrows of St. John's Harbour. The terrain atop the southside hills is surprisingly varied as picturesque ponds and sunken valleys alternate with bare hilltops and offer views of the Atlantic.

Follow the black and white trail markers across the top of the southside hills for about 3 kilometres. Next, you'll make a steep descent along Ennis River to the shores of Freshwater Bay. The trail follows the rocky barrier that separates Freshwater Pond, a lagoon, from Freshwater Bay. Storms have displaced many of the stepping stones that once facilitated this crossing; use caution here. Some wading may be necessary on the far side.

Much of the path from the rocky barrier to Blackhead is wooded but follows the cliff edge. At Small Point

the path turns sharply south, offering views of the coastline before arriving at the village of Blackhead.

 A barachois is a fresh or salt water lagoon behind a barrier of rock or sand. The barricade of large boulders that separates the freshwater lagoon from the ocean here is littered with the remains of sunken ships.

Distance:
10.6-kilometre linear trail

Trailheads: End of Southside Road, St. John's (47.33483, -52.405709); Blackhead (47.313394, -52.392604)

Highlights: Ocean views, barachois at Freshwater Bay

Elev. Range: 4–226 metres

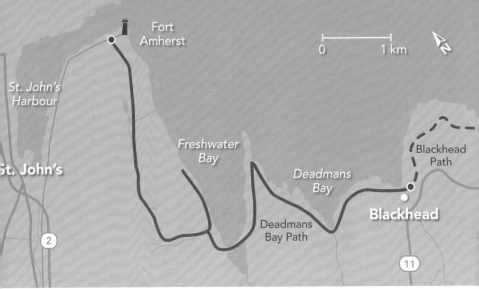

St. John's Harbour

Fort Amherst

St. John's

2

Freshwater Bay

Deadmans Bay

Deadmans Bay Path

Blackhead Path

Blackhead

11

0　　1 km

Trail maps are **not to be used for navigation.**

2 Blackhead to Cape Spear

This scenic path begins at the community of Blackhead and ends at the historic Cape Spear lighthouse, the most easterly point in North America. The path winds through blueberry grounds and climbs to a 100-metre-high headland. It provides sweeping views of Cape Spear to the south and Signal Hill to the north.

 There are two lighthouses at Cape Spear: one is currently active; the other has been restored as it was when it was inhabited by the Cantwell families. The restored premises are open to the public and provide insight into the solitary lives of lighthouse keepers and their families years ago.

Most of the path is exposed; on windy or foggy days we suggest choosing a different hike. In fine weather, though, it is a delightful walk, especially if a whale or two can be spotted below.

A dummy gun battery is at the halfway point of the hike. The battery or blind consists of stones stacked to form a circular defensive wall. On a warm day sit with a picnic lunch and enjoy the panoramic view.

Coming down off Blackhead, the trail passes Cantwell's Cove and then meanders to Cape Spear lighthouse, where generations of Cantwells lived and tended the light.

When you reach Cape Spear, take some time to explore the authentic gun batteries that were built to defend the coastline. Extreme caution should be taken here especially when high winds are blowing. Stay on the designated path.

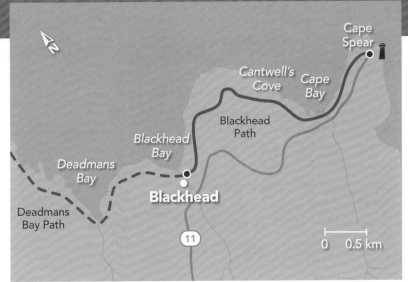

Trail maps are **not to be used for navigation.**

Distance:
3.7-kilometre linear trail

Trailheads: Blackhead (47.31339, -52.392604); Cape Spear light-house (47.31238, -52.37278)

Highlights: Views from the head-land summit, Cape Spear

Elev. Range: 5–121 metres

Cape Spear to Maddox Cove

Starting from Cape Spear, the path winds along clifftops and open headlands in a southerly direction until it reaches a deep gulch called The Basket. Two hundred metres farther is a junction in the trail, the high path to the south leads to North Head. This is an ideal spot for bird viewing, as seabirds are plentiful. In some winters this is a popular feeding ground for the majestic snowy owl. Follow the main trail almost due west.

The trail descends from the high ridge to a boardwalk that crosses a large boggy valley dotted, in season, with clusters of deep purple pitcher plants.

The terrain then changes; the trail crosses streams, passes numerous glacial erratics, and eventually enters thicker woods. The path frequently provides views of the rocky shoreline before it arrives at Maddox Cove.

 The pitcher plant is a carnivorous species. Its leaves are pitcher-shaped to hold water and enzymes which attract, and then digest, insects. The deep purple variety common to marshy areas has been adopted as Newfoundland and Labrador's provincial flower.

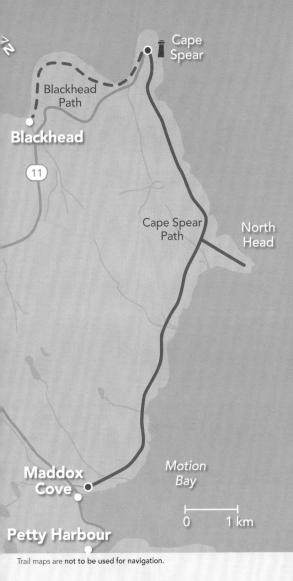

Cape Spear

Blackhead
Path

Blackhead

11

Cape Spear
Path

North
Head

Maddox
Cove

Motion
Bay

Petty Harbour

0   1 km

Trail maps are **not to be used for navigation.**

Distance: 10-kilometre linear trail

Trailheads: Cape Spear Lighthouse (47.311303, -52.372422); Maddox Cove (47.28227, -52.41572)

Highlights: Pitcher plants, The Basket, Motion Bay

Elev. Range: 7–64 metres

MOTION PATH

 ## Petty Harbour to Goulds

 This day-long hike begins with a 6-kilometre walk along Shoal Bay Road. The road is inland and uneven; we suggest starting the hike at the Shoal Bay trailhead and tackling it while your legs are fresh. It is also advisable to have a vehicle at both ends of the hike or at least transportation arranged before

 Petty Harbour, a traditional fishing village, has also gained fame as a location site for several television series (including *Hatching, Matching, and Dispatching* and *Republic of Doyle*) and movies (including *Orca* and *Rare Birds*).

Distance:
20-kilometre linear trail
(includes Shoal Bay Road)

Trailheads: Shoal Bay Road, Goulds (47.26086, -52.45278); Petty Harbour (south side, 47.27483, -52.42166)

Highlights: Motion Head, glacial erratics, wildflowers

Elev. Range: 2–212 metres

Campsite: Nipper's Cove

you start. Park in Goulds at the end of Shoal Bay Road past the bus turnaround. In Petty Harbour, park at the town hall on the north side or by the Fisherman's Centre on the south side.

The Shoal Bay access road joins the East Coast Trail at Raymond Head. The path turns north and follows the coastline near sea level for about 3 kilometres before ascending to Burkes Head. A campsite, consisting of tent platforms and an open-air privy, is located nearby at Nipper's Cove.

Eventually the path descends to near sea level at Motion Head. The swirling waters offshore give the path its name. Inland is an impressive field of large glacial erratics.

The trail turns northwest and climbs some 150 metres to the top of Big Hill before descending to the picturesque village of Petty Harbour.

Petty Harbour

Motion
Head

Motion
Path

Second
Pond

Lower
Cove

Third
Pond

10

Shoal Bay Road

Miner
Point

Shoal
Bay

Bay Bulls
Big Pond

Spout
Path

Trail maps are **not to be**
used for navigation.

0 1 km 2 km

4

Goulds to Bay Bulls

Spout Path, the longest segment of the East Coast Trail, requires a higher level of hiker fitness than most other sections. The hike is rated as strenuous, mainly due to its length (elevation gains are not substantial), but it is also one of the must-do hikes of the east coast of Newfoundland. It is not to be missed by anyone looking for spectacular ocean views and a challenging day on the trail.

It is best to begin this hike at Shoal Bay Road in Goulds. At Raymond Head, the path heads south and the Spout, for which this trail is named, is visible on a clear day from as far away as Long Point.

You are in for a few short climbs before the trail descends to the

 A spout may be created by a combination of wave action and freshwater streams running into gaps and holes in cliffs. They are found at several locations along the island's coastline. Heavy wave action can push water violently up these gaps or holes. The Spout along this trail can send a geyser 20 metres or more into the air in winter and summer.

Spout at about the halfway point of the hike. A nearby campsite at Little Bald Head has six tent platforms and an open-air privy.

After you pass through the campsite, there is still plenty to look forward to—sea stacks, an eagle's nest, and towering cliffs make this one of the most awe-inspiring hikes in the province. At the site of a resettled community at Freshwater, old house foundations are still visible and a waterfall follows long diagonal slabs of granite to the sea below.

The path turns west at North Head lighthouse eventually arriving at Gunridge, where a gravel road brings you to the parking area in Bay Bulls.

Trail maps are **not to be used for navigation**.

Distance:
23-kilometre linear trail

Trailheads: Shoal Bay Road, Goulds (47.26086, -52.45278); end of North Shore Road, Bay Bulls (47.18427, -52.46574)

Highlights: Water spout, sea stacks, lighthouse, whales

Elev. Range: 0–12 metres

Campsite: Little Bald Head

Bay Bulls to Witless Bay

If you are starting this hike from
Bay Bulls, drive to the end of Quays
Road on the south side of Bay Bulls
Harbour. A narrow road leads to the
path that winds through woods and
meadows and along the shore.

Mickeleens Path is not a difficult
hike, and it presents no great
elevation changes. It is peaceful, scenic, and colourful, with a
diversity of wildflowers throughout
the spring and summer. Interesting
place names along this path include
Mutton Cove, Long Harry Cove, and
Baboul Rocks.

Gull Island, which is in the Witless
Bay Seabird Ecological Reserve,
can be seen from Southern Head.

Whale and bird watching tour boats
out of Bay Bulls are a frequent sight
throughout the summer months.
Continue along the shoreline to
the trailhead at Bear Cove Road in
Witless Bay.

 Icebergs are floating giants calved
from glaciers in Greenland. The water
contained in the ice can be thousands
of years old. Companies in Newfoundland have capitalized on the purity
of this water and produce popular
bottled beverages such as water,
beer, and vodka from it. In late spring
icebergs drifting along the east coast
are sometimes brought close to shore
by wind and currents.

Distance:
7.3-kilometre linear trail

Trailheads: Quays Road, Bay
Bulls (47.18091, -52.48276);
Bear Cove Road, Witless Bay
(47.17067, -52.47537)

Highlights: Cliffs, coves,
Gull Island

Elev. Range: 25–70 metres

Spout
Path

**Bay
Bulls**

*Bay Bulls
Harbour*

Southern
Head

10

Bear Cove
Head

Gull
Island

**Witless
Bay**

*Witless
Bay*

0   1 km

Trail maps are **not to be used for navigation.**

1 Witless Bay to Mobile

Beginning in Witless Bay, this trail starts on Ragged Beach at the end of Gallows Cove Road. If you are walking north from Mobile, park at Mobile Central High School and cross Route 10 to the trailhead.

This path does not present any steep cliffs or demanding climbs. While pounding ocean waves can cause beach erosion—hikers should stay on the path for their own safety—this is an excellent walking trail year-round. We have been there on crisp clear winter days and the experience is exhilarating.

If you are travelling south from Ragged Beach, you can see Gull Island, a seabird ecological reserve. Farther along at Breaking Point

the path cuts through a tunnel of tuckamore, the stunted spruce trees characteristic of Newfoundland's windswept coastal headlands.

Several beaches are accessible from the path and are ideal places to stop and enjoy this beautiful coastline.

Tuckamore, also called tuckermore, tucken-more, or "tuck," are small stunted spruce and balsam fir trees frequently seen on exposed coastal areas in Newfoundland. In several places on the East Coast Trail, the path is a tunnel underneath a patch of tuckamore. In some places thick tuck-amore makes the trail impenetrable to humans, but provides an ideal habitat for rabbits and birds.

Distance:
7-kilometre linear trail

Trailheads: Ragged Beach, Witless Bay (47.154491, -52.484157); Mobile Beach, Mobile (47.145641, -52.503080)

Highlights: Seabirds, beaches

Elev. Range: Minimal change

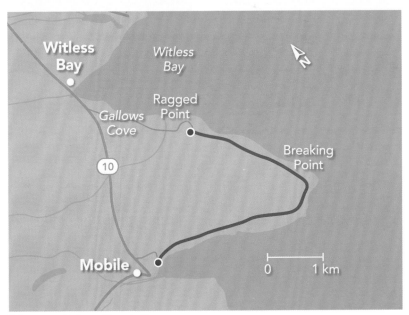

Trail maps are **not to be used** for navigation.

Mobile to Tors Cove

Only 5 kilometres long, this trail can easily be done as an out-and-back hike or combined with the Beaches Path Trail for a longer hike. Park at the end of Cod Seine Cove Road in Mobile or at the Church of the Sacred Heart in Tors Cove.

This is a gentle low-lying path with little elevation change, which makes it ideal for children and first-time hikers. Stretches of trail pass through the woods, with occasional access to small rocky beaches. Tinkers Point, with its meadows and ocean views, is a perfect rest spot. "Tinker" is the local name for the razorbill, a seabird similar in size and colouring to the common murre.

When you enter Tors Cove, you will pass an iconic image of Newfoundland, the Cribbies, a clapboarded saltbox house. Below the house lies a beautiful grassy headland and beach. Just offshore is a small island where grazing sheep can sometimes be seen.

The path leads uphill from the beach and goes directly to Sacred Heart Church and car park.

 Although this path is named for the razorbill, hikers are more likely to see common murres or turres, as they are often called. Large colonies exist on Baccalieu Island, Cape St. Mary's, and at the Witless Bay Seabird Reserve.

Distance:
5-kilometre linear trail

Trailheads: Cod Seine Cove Road, Mobile (47.14249, -52.495809); Sacred Heart Church, Tors Cove (47.12525, -52.504408)

Highlights: Tinkers Point, Tors Cove Beach

Elev. Range: 0–28 metres

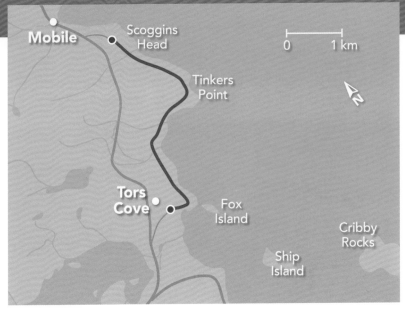

Trail maps are **not** to be used for navigation.

★ The saltbox house is seen in many places in Newfoundland and is also popular on the eastern seaboard of the United States. It generally has a steep sloping roof, usually showing two floors from the front view then sloping sharply to show one storey at the back. It is so named because it mimics the shape of the boxes that were used to ship salt to the province. In modified saltbox-style houses, the roofline at the back half of the house has been given a more shallow pitch than the front, extending the house to provide more living space. The Cribbies displays this shallow pitch modification.

1 Bauline East to La Manche

Hikers may walk the 4-kilometre path from Bauline East into the former settlement of La Manche (French for "the sleeve"), explore the area, and return along the same path. However, from the parking area at the end of La Manche Road a 1-kilometre trail links to the old village site, so, with a vehicle parked at each end, a return trip can be avoided.

Park at the wharf in Bauline East. A gravel road brings you uphill to the start of the trail. Most of the trail is in woods but, like on many of the East Coast Trails, signposts indicate several points of interest just off the main trail. Depending on your mood, time constraints, and energy levels, you should take advantage of exploring as many of them as possible; that unusual ocean view, eagles nest, or waterfall view may just be an experience to remember. Doctors Cove on this trail is just such a place.

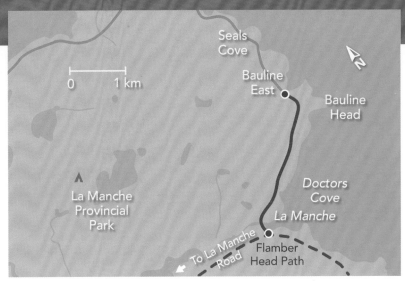

Trail maps are **not to be used for navigation.**

La Manche village was nestled at the head of the narrow inlet surrounded by high hills. La Manche River flows in a torrent through a narrow gorge into the bay from Lower Pond. In 1961, the population was 25 people. A severe storm in 1966 destroyed all of the fishing stages, and the village was subsequently abandoned. Many house foundations are still visible.

Stone walls and the outlines of gardens can still be seen. Bridges over the river have been replaced at least four times. In 1999, the ECTA built an impressive 45-metre-long suspension bridge, held in place by thick steel cables bolted into solid rock.

Whales, seals, and even sea otters are occasionally seen in this peaceful cove.

Distance:
5-kilometre linear trail

Trailheads: Bauline East wharf (47.104788, -52.503962); end of La Manche Road, off Route 10 (47.100215, -52.530564)

Highlights: Suspension bridge, old settlement, Doctors Cove

Elev. Range: 2–64 metres

Camping:
La Manche Provincial Park

La Manche to Brigus South

This 12-kilometre path is more difficult than the East Coast Trail sections immediately to the north, but the extra effort is rewarded with exceptional views.

The term *outport* comes from England and refers to a coastal settlement outside a large city like St. John's.

Cape Neddick, a high headland just off the main trail, is worth the climb. The same is true of Flamber Head, which rises to 60 metres. In between these two headlands are the rock formations at Gentleman's Head—squared chunks of rock resembling huge piles of dark chocolate, but more precisely eroded grey shale and sandstone of the St. John's Group. The nearby waterfall at the Quays is a popular place to take a lunch break or to cool your feet. This river flows eastward from Little Pond, which has several beaver lodges, so it is advisable not to drink the water before either filtering or boiling it. This is good advice to follow on any of the trails in the province.

A site to pitch tents is found at Roaring Cove, near the halfway point of the path. The nearby sea stacks and the grassy hillside leading up Flamber Head make for great photography. This was one of the major campsites for the ECTA building crews while constructing the trail to the north and south of Flamber Head.

Proceeding south from Roaring Cove the path is fairly wooded until it emerges at the picturesque outport of Brigus South.

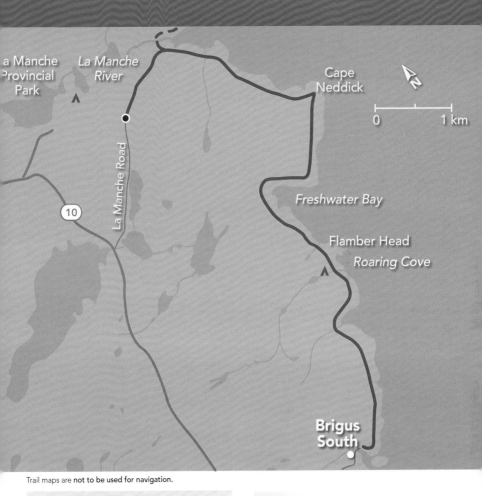

Trail maps are **not to be used for navigation.**

Distance:
12-kilometre linear trail

Trailheads: La Manche Village
(park at end of La Manche Road,
47.100215, -52.530564); Brigus
South (47.065207, -52.525719)

Highlights: Cape Neddick,
Flamber Head, the Quays

Elev. Range: 2–96 metres

Camping: Roaring Cove

Brigus South to Admiral's Cove

From Brigus South, the path climbs from near sea level to about 50 metres and more or less stays on this height of land until Tar Cove Point. Several side trails to viewpoints at Herring Cove Beach and Tar Cove Point are worth checking out.

Along with its curious name, Hares Ears Point offers an outstanding view. Cross Cove and Doctors Rock are two other viewpoints not to be missed. The path ends at Cranes Lane in Admiral's Cove.

This path can be hiked as a loop thanks to a cart track that was once part of the old Southern Shore Highway. This cart track is clearly marked on the ECTA map; it is easy to follow but not maintained and could be wet.

The parking areas are clearly marked in both communities.

 Brigus South was originally called Brigus, but this name was changed in the 1920s to avoid confusing it with the town of the same name in Conception Bay.

Distance: 6.5-kilometre linear trail or 8-kilometre loop

Trailheads: Brigus South, west side of harbour (47.06434, -52.53013); Admiral's Cove, Cranes Lane (47.060512, -52.534693)

Highlights:
Whales in summer, loop hike

Elev. Range: 3–50 metres

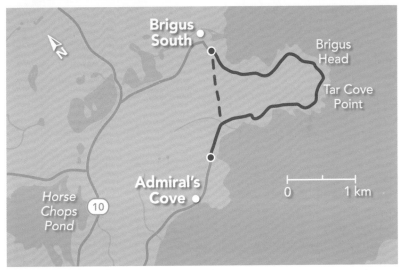

Trail maps are **not to be used for navigation**.

④ Cape Broyle to Calvert

This may be the most difficult section of the East Coast Trail. Even getting to the trailheads is a challenge. ECTA advises that only experienced hikers should attempt this trail and all hikers should bring survival tools and be aware that this hike could take an entire day.

At Cape Broyle, park on the un-paved portion of the Ultramar Gas Station parking lot. Walk to the end of the South Side Road to the cul de sac. Go down to the beach and walk east for several minutes. Follow black and white markers to the trail proper. This trail is mostly wooded until, at approximately 12 kilometres, at Church Cove

The town of Calvert is named for George Calvert. The Colony of Avalon was established in his name in 1621, even though he did not visit the colony until 1627. He was subsequently granted land by Charles I of England in the Chesapeake Bay region, which became the Colony of Maryland, where he settled permanently with his family. The colony of Avalon endured, however, and was one of the earliest permanent English settlements in North America.

Meadow it opens to an ocean view. At Cape Broyle Head the trail turns south toward Calvert.

To start at the southern trailhead, turn left off Route 10 at Power's Store in Calvert. Drive to the end of the pavement about 4 kilometres, then 1 kilometre on a dirt road to the trailhead sign. From the Calvert trailhead, the hike begins with a rigorous climb to the top of Cape Broyle Head, which provides views of the coastline and the Ferryland lighthouse. The path proceeds along the ridge to North Head and then turns west and follows the clifftops high above Cape Broyle Bay.

A side trail leads down to the sandy beach at Lance Cove. A little farther along the main trail is the Long Will campsite. It is about 7 kilometres from the campsite to the trailhead in Cape Broyle.

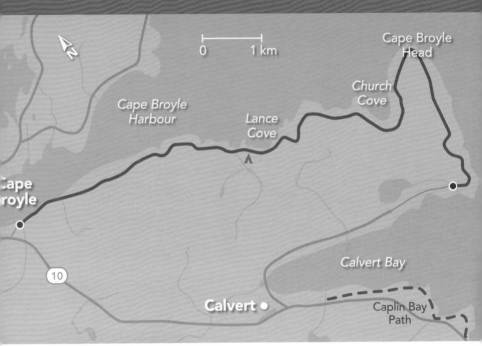

Trail maps are **not to be used for navigation.**

Distance: 18.5 kilometres

Trailheads: South Side Road, Cape Broyle (47.051959, -52.564554); 1 kilometre past end of paved road, north side of Calvert (47.030208, -52.514872)

Highlights: View of Ferryland, Lance Cove beach

Elev. Range: 0–160 metres

Campsite: Long Will Point

Calvert to Ferryland

The north trailhead for Caplin Bay path is 1 kilometre south of Power's Store in Calvert. From the trailhead, the main path descends into the woods and soon comes to a side trail to a beach at Deep Cove. The main path continues past the Catholic cemetery and eventually arrives at Ferryland.

After the path crosses Route 10, it goes to the top of Fox Hill, from where there is a sweeping view of the harbour, islands, and the Ferryland lighthouse. The trail descends the hill past an old graveyard just above the Colony of Avalon Interpretation Centre.

This short hike allows time for the hiker to visit the centre and the dig site. If you have time, walk out to the lighthouse. Gourmet picnic

 Archaeologists from Memorial University have been working at the Colony of Avalon dig site since the 1980s. Their discoveries reveal a complex and well-developed working colony with mansion house, forge, warehouses, dock, cobble roads, and gardens. Thousands of the recovered artifacts are beautifully displayed in the Interpretation Centre.

lunches are available at Lighthouse Picnics on Ferryland Head. It is usually necessary to book in advance.

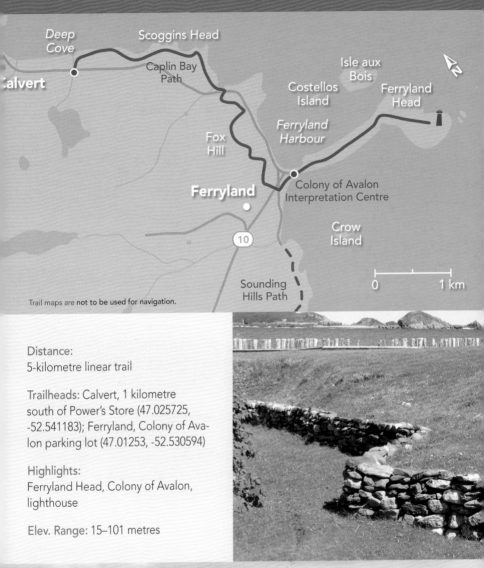

Deep
Cove

Scoggins Head

Calvert

Caplin Bay
Path

Isle aux
Bois

Costellos
Island

Ferryland
Head

Fox
Hill

Ferryland
Harbour

Colony of Avalon
Interpretation Centre

Ferryland

Crow
Island

10

Sounding
Hills Path

0   1 km

Distance:
5-kilometre linear trail

Trailheads: Calvert, 1 kilometre
south of Power's Store (47.025725,
-52.541183); Ferryland, Colony of Avalon parking lot (47.01253, -52.530594)

Highlights:
Ferryland Head, Colony of Avalon,
lighthouse

Elev. Range: 15–101 metres

Ferryland to Aquaforte

 "Community links," such as those between this trail and Mudder Wet Path, are found on many of the East Coast trails. They are basically sections of road or highway between beginnings or ends of trails that often run through towns. Services and amenities are often available along these road links and they can be an enjoyable part of the hiking experience.

Distance: 6.5-kilometre linear trail (including paved lane in Ferryland)

Trailheads: Colony of Avalon parking lot, Ferryland (47.01253, -52.530594); Spout River Bridge, Route 10 (47.004433, -52.555936)

Highlights: View from Sounding Hills, Spout River

Elev. Range: 3–80 metres

From the Colony of Avalon parking lot, head south on foot along a paved lane for about 1 kilometre. At the end of the pavement, the trail enters the woods and winds for 2 kilometres to the top of Sounding Hills. The summit offers views of Ferryland Head, Aquaforte Harbour, and Spurwink Island.

Farther along the trail is Stony River and then Spout River with its powerful current funnelling between large boulders on its way to the ocean.

The path follows the bank of the river for about 500 metres before emerging at the Southern Shore Highway (Route 10). The designated parking area for this trailhead is just north of the bridge. If you continue to the Mudder Wet Path, you will have to walk on the road for approximately 3 kilometres. Care should be taken to face oncoming traffic until you meet the head of the next trail at the end of the pavement in the community of Aquaforte.

Caplin Bay
Path

Ferryland ○

10

Crow
Island

Sounding
Hills Path

Spurwink
Island

0   1 km

Aquaforte
Harbour

Trail maps are **not to be used for navigation.**

1 Aquaforte to South West River

This is a gentle little loop hike. Start from the trailhead by the parking area just south of Hagan's Hospitality Home on Route 10. (The northern trailhead for the Spurwink Island Path is also at this parking area, so be sure to take the correct path.)

You will be first impressed by the beautiful Aquaforte River, also called South West River. Viewpoints allow for easy observation of the South West River gorge. The path descends to sea level; follow the shoreline 1 kilometre to the Little River estuary. If it is not possible to wade across the estuary, take the trail on the west side of the river and follow it around to the other side of Little River.

The path proceeds up the north bank of Little River to another waterfall, which is not as spectacular as the one in the Aquaforte River but quite beautiful nonetheless. At this point you have to return along the riverbank and climb the steps to the top of Sally's Hill.

From the top of Sally's Hill, either take the path to the right toward the trailhead at Aquaforte or turn left and head back to the parking area on Route 10.

A tidal estuary is an area where the widening channel of the river enters the sea. Tidal differences can pose dangerous situations if crossing the channel is called for on a section of a hike. Strong currents, fast-flowing water, and very cold water are not to be underestimated.

Distance: 3-kilometre loop

Trailhead: Route 10, just south of Hagan's Hospitality Home (47.004154, -52.590000)

Highlights: Waterfalls, river gorge, estuary

Elev. Range: 0–80 metres

Little
River

Aquaforte

10

Aquaforte
Harbour

Mudder
Wet Path

Spurwink
Island Path

Aquaforte
River

Trail maps are **not** to be used for navigation.

0   1 km

South West River to Port Kirwan

This is a long trail with difficult sections; allow a full day to complete the hike. One trailhead is on Route 10 just south of Hagan's Hospitality Home, close to the Mudder Wet trailhead; the other is at the church in Port Kirwan near Fermeuse.

From the Immaculate Conception Church in Port Kirwan, walk about 500 metres along the old lane to Clear Cove, where you'll find a beautiful meadow and beach. Follow trail signs north along the coastline to Berry Head, about 7 kilometres farther. The Berry Head sea arch is not only the outstanding feature of this path but it is also one of the most unexpected, awe-inspiring sights on the entire East Coast Trail. You may want to climb the arch but care should be taken as erosion is always ongoing. About 500 metres past the arch you will arrive at South Head with a view of Spurwink Island and across the bay to the Ferryland lighthouse.

The path turns westward and follows the coastline of the deep fjord-like harbour of Aquaforte. After it passes a campsite at Gallows Cove, the trail enters deep woods before emerging onto heathland for the last kilometre to the trailhead on Route 10.

Spurwink Island

Gallows
Cove

Berry
Head

Mudder
Wet Path

Aquaforte

Spurwink
Island Path

Clear
Cove

Port
Kirwan

10

Fermeuse
Harbour

Fermeuse

Kingman's Cove

Bear Cove
Point Path

0   1 km

Trail maps are **not to be used for navigation.**

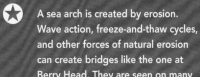 A sea arch is created by erosion. Wave action, freeze-and-thaw cycles, and other forces of natural erosion can create bridges like the one at Berry Head. They are seen on many shorelines around the province and are always points of great interest.

Distance:
17-kilometre linear trail

Trailheads: Route 10, south of Aquaforte (just south of Mudder Wet trailhead) (47.004154, -52.59000); church in Port Kirwan (46.580989, -52.543397)

Highlights: Berry Head sea arch, Spurwink Island

Elev. Range: 7–79 metres

Campsite: Gallows Cove

2

Kingman's Cove to Renews

This path begins at the end of the pavement in Kingman's Cove on the south side of Fermeuse Harbour. At the beginning of the trail remains of the remains of the *Ilex*, sunk in 1948, are still visible offshore. One kilometre into the trail, a side trail leads to Trix's Cove, a blueberry picker's mecca. Remains of the former community are still visible.

Much of the path passes through woods until it reaches Bear Cove Point, where there is an automated light and foghorn. This is approximately the halfway point of this hike and a perfect spot for a boil-up. Five hundred metres farther is South Point, with a lookout where you can view the jagged sea stacks in Southern Cove.

Bear Cove Point Path stays close to the coastline as it proceeds south and finally turns west after passing Sculpin Bay and crossing a large meadow to the historic town of Renews.

> ★ Archaeologists have discovered building sites dating to the 17th century in Renews.
>
> The English and French fought over this area because of the valuable fishing grounds.

Distance: 11.5 kilometres

Trailheads: End of the pavement, Kingman's Cove (46.575236, -52.554942); the Mount, Renews (park at church or museum, 46.551936, -52.55511)

Highlights: Bear Cove Point, South Point, Trix's Cove, town of Renews

Elev. Range: 11–56 metres

Port Kirwan

Sleepers Point

Fermeuse Harbour

Bear Cove Point

Fermeuse

Kingman's Cove

Bear Cove Pond

South Point

10

Sculpin Point

0   1 km

Renews

Trail maps are **not to be used for navigation.**

2 Renews to Cappahayden

This trail, which begins at the end of the pavement on the south side of Renews Harbour, is fairly level for the first 2 kilometres, at which point it reaches Renews Head and a 50-metre climb. The path stays along this ridge for about 1 kilometre before descending to near sea level. Renews Island is about 2 kilometres south of Renews Head; a colony of cormorants nests on the island during the summer.

At Bear Cove, you will cross a bridge and then follow a dirt road for a short distance before taking a footpath back toward the beach. The path remains low and close to the coastline all the way to Cappahayden.

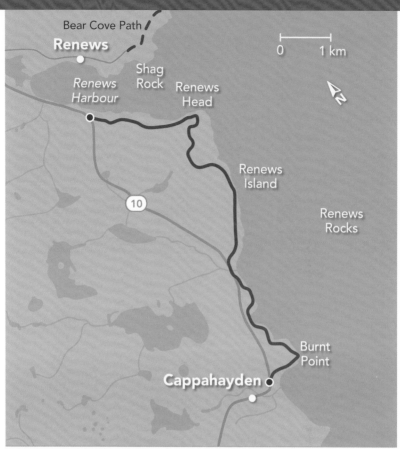

Bear Cove Path

Renews

Renews
Harbour

Shag
Rock

Renews
Head

Renews
Island

Renews
Rocks

10

Burnt
Point

Cappahayden

0   1 km

Trail maps are **not to be used for navigation.**

Perhaps no part of the province celebrates its Irish heritage more than the area south of St. John's known as the Southern Shore. Irish immigration to Newfoundland peaked in the early 1800s, and many of the newcomers settled in the fishing communities strung along this section of the Avalon, which is part of the Irish Loop. It is still possible to meet people whose history here goes back generations yet their accents remain indistinguishable from their forebears in Waterford County.

Distance:
10-kilometre linear trail

Trailheads: End of pavement, south side of Renews Harbour (46.545659, -52.561147); Lawlor's Road, Cappahayden (46.513846, -52.564196)

Highlights: Renews Island

Elev. Range: 3–76 metres

BONAVISTA PENINSULA

Bonavista, the town that gives this peninsula its name, is where John Cabot reputedly made landfall after crossing the Atlantic from Bristol, England, in 1497. Cabot returned home with news that the waters around Newfoundland were teeming with cod, reporting that "the schools of codfish [there] were so thick you [could] walk on their backs." Fishermen from Spain, Portugal, the Basque Country, France, and England were soon making regular visits.

The Ryan Premises, a former fishing merchant's store and warehouse complex in the town of Bonavista, has been converted into a fascinating museum that clearly depicts the role of the cod fishery in shaping Newfoundland's history.

Another must-see is Port Union, a community created by the Fishermen's Protective Union under the leadership of William Coaker, one of Newfoundland's unique historical figures. Coaker brought modern advances to Port Union, including electrification, making it the first settlement outside of St. John's to be so served.

Trinity's many beautifully preserved houses and commercial buildings make a visit to this community seem like a step into the past. Architecture is not the only attraction: Summer in the Bight, a vibrant theatre festival held every year in Trinity, highlights the works of Newfoundland playwrights in nightly performances throughout the summer season.

The Bonavista Peninsula has numerous hiking trails of various lengths. Geology, history, coastal scenery, and wildlife ensure that these trails will not disappoint hikers of any fitness level. Moose, fox, whales, and seabirds are abundant, as are wildflowers, an attraction on any trail.

The Bonavista Peninsula has been fashioned into a tourist destination in recent years, with many B&Bs, cottages, inns, and fine restaurants, including the Bonavista Social Club in Upper Amherst Cove, Fishers' Loft and Two Whales Coffee Shop in Port Rexton, and The Twine Loft in Trinity.

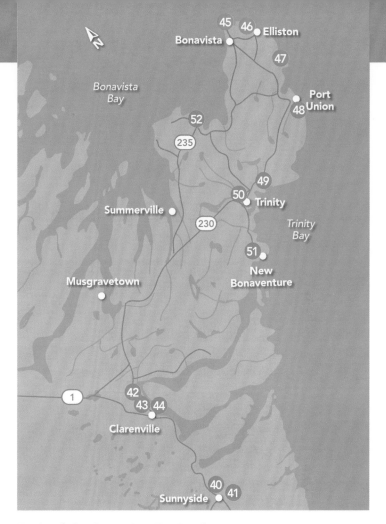

Trails of the Bonavista Peninsula

40. Centre Hill Trail / Sunnyside
41. Truce Sound Peace Garden Trail / Sunnyside
42. Bare Mountain Trail / Clarenville
43. Rotary/Wellness Trails / Clarenville
44. Shoal Harbour Loop / Clarenville
45. Dungeon to Cape Bonavista / Bonavista
46. Klondike Trail / Elliston to Spillar's Cove
47. Little Catalina to Maberly Trail / Little Catalina to Maberly
48. Lodge's Pond to Murphy's Cove Trail / Melrose to Port Union
49. Fox Island Trail / Champney's West
50. Skerwink Trail / Trinity East
51. British Harbour Trail / New Bonaventure to British Harbour
52. King's Cove Lighthouse Trail / King's Cove

Sunnyside

Volcanoes aren't generally associated with Newfoundland, but the large hill behind the town of Sunnyside was formed by an ancient volcano. With an elevation of 384 metres, it is the highest point in eastern Newfoundland, and a great hike. The Sunnyside town council has named this a "wilderness trail" as it can no longer maintain the boardwalk across such a long stretch of bog. Hikers should be prepared for wet and muddy sections.

Near the end of the main road through the town, you will arrive at the well-marked trailhead and parking area. Curiously, the hill that is visible from the Trans-Canada Highway is completely out of sight and remains so for much of the early part of the hike.

The trail climbs gradually, crosses a river, wends through forest, passes an old log cabin, and crosses large barrens. A freshwater spring and tent platforms are located beside a pond at the base of the hill.

From this point, the summit is only 400 metres, but it is a steep climb and the toughest part of the hike. The 360-degree panorama from the top, however, makes the effort worthwhile—all the more reason to do this trail on a sunny day with high visibility.

In the 1930s, a fire tower was built at the summit because of the constant threat of forest fires from steam locomotives. It has been replaced by a small gazebo, well anchored against strong and unrelenting winds.

Distance: 5-kilometre linear trail (10-kilometre return)

Trailhead: End of main road in Sunnyside (47.511925, -53.525884)

Highlights: Outstanding views from summit

Elev. range: 1–384 metres

Walk back the way you came, enjoying the view of Placentia Bay to the south.

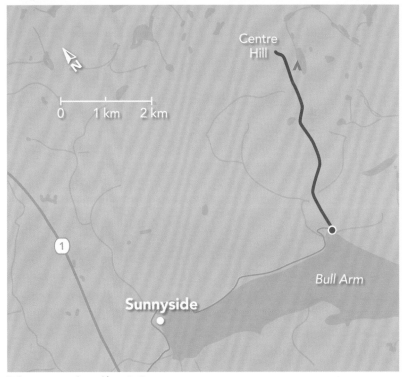

Trail maps are **not to be used for navigation.**

Sunnyside

Hikers familiar with the Centre Hill Trail in Sunnyside may be tempted to overlook a shorter and less challenging trail in this community. The Truce Sound Peace Garden Trail, at 1.5 kilometres in length, could be dismissed as just a "dawdle"—but this would be a mistake.

Short it may be, but this path follows the shoreline of Truce Sound and is a pleasant walk through boreal forest with a unique destination. From a lookout, a teepee constructed of bleached white "longers" can be seen approximately half a kilometre away. At first glance, it seems that the teepee is on an island, and you might wonder if (and how) you're going to get to your destination without becoming wet. Fortunately, a narrow spit of sand or tombolo provides a safe and dry passage to tiny Frenchman's Island. Once across, go left along the shoreline to the Peace Garden memorial.

Frenchman's Island was the site of a November 6, 1612, meeting between members of John Guy's colony at Cupids and a group of Beothuk. It was a peaceful event that involved the sharing of gifts and food and was intended to mark the beginning of a mutually beneficial relationship. Unfortunately, it was not to be, and the ultimate fate of the Beothuk people lends a solemn poignancy to the site.

Tombolo is an Italian word for one or more sandbars formed by wave action that connect an island to the mainland. A lagoon can be formed by two tombolos that eventually fill with sediment. A tombolo can be a form of peninsula.

A *longer* is a long tapering pole, usually a conifer, with bark left on, used in constructing roofs, floors, or surfaces of stages and flakes. (Source: *Dictionary of Newfoundland English*)

Distance: 5-kilometre linear trail (10-kilometre return)

Trailhead: End of main road in Sunnyside (47.511925, -53.525884)

Highlights: Outstanding views from summit

Elev. range: 1–384 metres

Sunnyside

0   0.4 km

Frenchman's Island

Trail maps are **not to be used for navigation.**

1

Clarenville

Hikers may choose to begin this trail from one of two starting points: the Professional Building on Manitoba Drive in Clarenville (at the north end of the parking lot) or Hunt's Hill near the Shoal Harbour causeway. This trail can be walked as a linear trail (if you park a vehicle at each end) or as a loop.

 In July 1933, in an effort to demonstrate Italy's pre-World War II air power, 20 S-55 flying boats under the command of General Italo Balbo landed on the waters of Random Sound. At the time, it was the largest fleet of aircraft to successfully complete a transatlantic flight.

Distance: 3-kilometre linear trail

Trailhead: Parking lot, Professional Building, Manitoba Drive (48.094706, -53.582545); Hunt's Hill near Shoal Harbour causeway (48.105301, -53.583487)

Highlights: Ponds, forest, view from lookout

Elev. range: 20–140 metres

The highlight of the trail is, unquestionably, the spectacular view from the lookout at the top of the appropriately named Bare Mountain. On a fine day, Random Island and the town of Clarenville, separated by the sparkling waters of Random Sound, present a splendid vista. A substantial viewing platform, equipped with affixed binoculars, provides a comfortable place from which to take photos, hydrate, and take off or add a layer of clothing. A signpost on site gives directions and distances to various places in the province.

From the Bare Mountain Lookout the trail continues in a northerly direction over The Dam to the causeway in Shoal Harbour. If you don't have a vehicle at the Shoal Harbour trailhead, you may prefer to loop back around Stanley's Pond and return to the trailhead at Manitoba Drive.

The route winds through thick boreal forest but frequent signs make the path easy to follow. Watch for ospreys and other raptors.

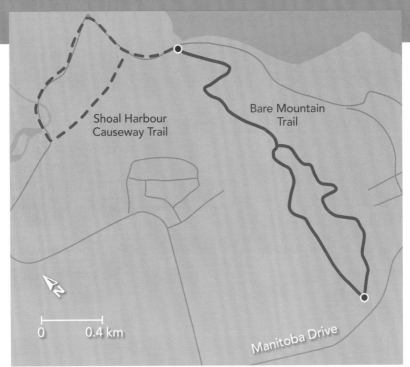

Shoal Harbour
Causeway Trail

Bare Mountain
Trail

Manitoba Drive

0   0.4 km

Trail maps are **not to be used for navigation.**

Clarenville

Trail builders in Clarenville have cleverly connected Rotary Trail and Wellness Trail so that they can be walked separately or linked together for a longer hike. The trails can be accessed from several trailheads; the hike can be as long or as short as you wish.

Begin where Memorial Drive meets Cormack Drive at the bridge over Lower Shoal Harbour River, which flows into Lower Shoal Harbour and then into Random Sound. The trail follows the left bank of Lower Shoal Harbour River past Elizabeth Swan Memorial Park, crosses the river near the confluence with Dark Hole Brook, and continues west.

While you are meandering through the lush boreal forest, it is easy to forget that you are still inside the Clarenville town limits. The path

proceeds in a westerly direction for about 1.5 kilometres before turning north and linking up with the Newfoundland Trailway. From this point you can return to the starting point or join the Wellness Trail for a longer walk.

The Wellness Trail emerges from the woods and passes by two schools and through a busy commercial area before joining the Newfoundland Trailway. For a longer hike, cross Manitoba Drive and connect with Bare Mountain Trail (see hike 42).

There are helpful signs along the trail and trails are well maintained. An excellent brochure on the Clarenville Trail System is available at the Tourist Information Centre.

Distance: 3–6 kilometres

Trailhead: Memorial Drive Bridge (48.090534, -53.574422)

Highlights: Boreal forest, rivers

Elev. range: 3–90 metres

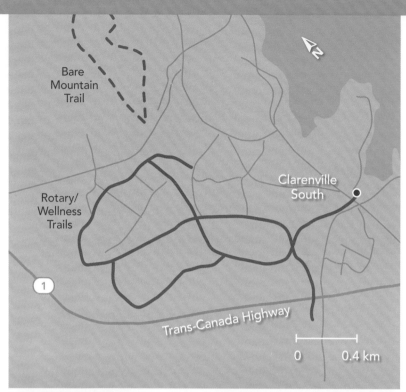

Bare
Mountain
Trail

Clarenville
South

Rotary/
Wellness
Trails

1

Trans-Canada Highway

0   0.4 km

Trail maps are **not to be used for navigation.**

Clarenville/Shoal Harbour

There are many places to begin this hike, but we suggest parking either just across the bridge where the Shoal Harbour River runs into the harbour, or farther along Harbour Drive near Hunt's Hill by a viewing platform. A large map of the route is posted at the base of the stairway below the viewing platform on Memorial Drive near the start of the causeway.

This is an urban walk with a difference. It features an impressive walkway parallel to the causeway, offering a close-up view of the harbour, home to Canada geese, osprey, and eagles. Across Smith Sound is Random Island.

At the other side of the causeway, the path crosses Harbour Drive and turns left, eventually crossing Shoal Harbour River, where the river rushes into the harbour. From this point, turn onto Cedar Crescent and then quickly take a left onto the path. This will bring you to a viewing platform which has signboards detailing some of the history of the area, including the landing of an Italian seaplane fleet under the command of Captain Balbo in 1933.

 The Town of Clarenville is recognized as a Canada Goose sanctuary thanks to the initiative of Clyde Tuck of Shoal Harbour, who brought two tame geese and one wild goose to the area in 1922. Large flocks can be seen in the area each spring and autumn.

Distance: 3-kilometre loop

Trailhead: Viewing platform, Harbour Drive (48.105700, -53.584107); Shoal Harbour River bridge (48.105506, -53.591363)

Highlights: Wildlife, harbour views, lookout

Elev. range: 3–25 metres

Should you wish an extended hike, the northern trailhead of the Bare Mountain Trail is 50 metres farther along the Newfoundland Trailway.

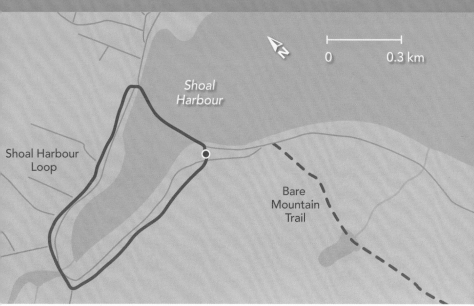

Trail maps are **not to be used** for navigation.

Bonavista

This gentle hike links two of the most dramatic sights on the Bonavista Peninsula: the Dungeon and Cape Bonavista. Dungeon Provincial Park features a collapsed sea cave that was once, in fact, two distinct caves. Erosion and the collapse of the cave ceiling created an enormous sinkhole, exposing two arches and allowing the ocean to flow in.

From the Dungeon, the trail travels north along the Trinity Bay side of the peninsula for approximately 2 kilometres, then crosses the Cape Shore Road on the Bonavista Bay side. It goes through a community pasture, where horses and cattle roam freely. If you would rather avoid these animals, pick up the Cape Shore Trail and walk to Cape Bonavista on the Bonavista Bay side.

During the spring and summer, the trail may offer opportunities to see icebergs and whales. Nearing Cape Bonavista, the trail comes to a large bronze statue of John Cabot. The trail officially ends at the Cape Bonavista lighthouse, but plan to spend some time bird watching and exploring the surrounding area.

The Cape Bonavista lighthouse, completed in 1843, has a circular stone tower surrounded by a two-storey wood-frame structure. The light was traditionally fuelled by seal oil, which left a residue on the glass (frequent hand-polishing was required to clean the glass). The lighthouse has been turned into a museum which depicts the typical life of its keeper in the 1800s.

Distance:
7-kilometre linear trail

Trailheads: Dungeon Provincial Park (48.400076, -53.050293); Cape Bonavista lighthouse (48.415265, -53.0500638)

Highlights: The Dungeon, lighthouse, Cabot statue, and whale, iceberg, and puffin sightings

Elev. range: 2–20 metres

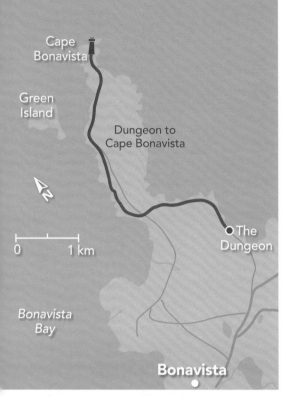

Cape
Bonavista

Green
Island

Dungeon to
Cape Bonavista

N

0   1 km

The
Dungeon

Bonavista
Bay

Bonavista

Trail maps are **not to be used for navigation.**

Elliston to Spillar's Cove

With over 100 visible root cellars, Elliston has been dubbed the "root cellar capital of the world." Wander through the town to check out the many fine examples and even take a peek inside one or two. The community also has a sealer's museum and a memorial to the sealing disasters of 1914.

After visiting these sites, explore the Klondike Trail from the north end of Elliston to Spillar's Cove.

The trail goes over L'Argent Hill and then past a cove full of sea stacks and jagged rocks. A track goes directly to the community of Spillar's Cove, but if you take this route you will miss out on a highlight of the area—an island with a colony of puffins. To see the puffin colony, follow the shoreline (instead of the dirt track); there is no developed path, and the terrain is uneven.

If you miss the puffins along the Klondike Trail, be sure to check out the puffin sanctuary on Bird Island on the main road between Elliston and Maberly. Sit for a few minutes and watch them fly off to search for food and then return to feed their young, hidden from predatory gulls, deep in their burrows.

Continue to follow the coastline into Spillar's Cove.

Distance: 5-kilometre loop around headland

Trailhead: Elliston (north end, 48.382870, -53.033240)

Highlights: Sea stacks, puffin rock

Elev. range: 34–60 metres

 Puffins can dive to depths of 60 metres in search of small fish and crustaceans to feed their young. They are sometimes called sea parrots because of their large orange bills. At about seven weeks, the young puffins, now able to feed themselves, leave their burrows.

Sea stacks are pillars of rock which stand apart from the coastline. These impressive formations are formed by coastal erosion caused by wind, waves, and the freezing and thawing of water in the cracks and faultlines of the rocks.

Trail maps are **not to be used for navigation.**

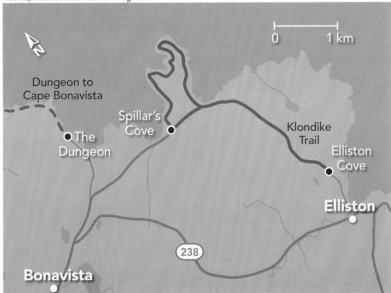

Little Catalina to Maberly

Allow a full day for this coastal hike which connects two Trinity Bay communities. The route is marked by black and white stakes but, as little maintenance has been done in recent years, these may not all be in place. The path hugs the coast for most of the way. There could be muddy sections if the weather has been wet.

> ★ The name Catalina is said to derive from *Cataluna*, the Spanish name for St. Catherine.

Maberly, just south of Elliston, also has root cellars. Now a curiosity and tourist attraction, these were once essential for preserving root crops through the fall and winter. A root cellar had to be well-constructed, dry, rodent-proof, and deep enough to keep the crops from freezing.

As you leave Maberly, look for several gazes or blinds used by seabird hunters—this area has been frequented by hunters and berry pickers for generations.

The terrain becomes more dramatic as you travel southward, with steeper cliffs and more trees. Much of this long trail goes through heathland and includes a variety of plant life, including blueberries, partridgeberries, and crowberries. Charlie's Cove is the site of a former settlement and a perfect spot to stop for refreshments.

The trail crosses bare, rocky terrain as it enters Little Catalina.

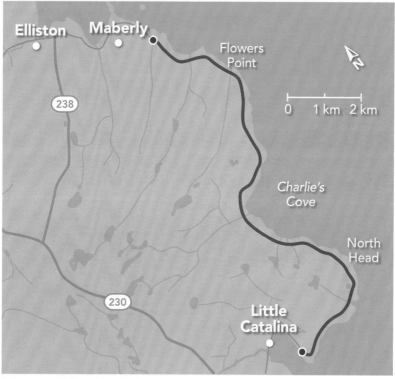

Trail maps are **not to be used for navigation.**

Distance: 17 kilometres

Trailheads: Maberly
(48.370937, -53.004760);
Little Catalina (48.322945,
-53.020743)

Highlights: Cliffs and coves

Elev. range: 2–49 metres

Melrose to Port Union

Although this trail officially begins in Port Union next to St. Catherine's Haven (see red dotted line on map), we suggest starting at the northern end of Melrose for additional sightseeing. This well-worn scenic hike follows the shoreline of Trinity Bay and connects with the main trail at Back Cove.

From Back Cove, the trail makes its way to Burnt Point. Here you will find a viewing platform and a comfortable bench facing east to the lighthouse on Green Island directly opposite, one of the few manned lighthouses left in the province.

From Burnt Point, the trail follows the shoreline of Catalina Harbour. Look for roseroot plants along this section of the trail. About halfway back to Port Union is Murphy's Cove, once a fishing and farming settlement. The road that linked

 Look for roseroot plants, also called "live-forever," in the rock crevices of this trail. Roseroot's waxy coating, a natural secretion, is a vital defense against the salt spray on the sea cliffs, where it thrives. It is an edible plant.

Distance:
8.5-kilometre linear trail

Trailheads: Melrose
(48.290724, -53.034920); Port Union (48.294262, -53.043426)

Highlights: Shoreline, Green Island lighthouse

Elev. range: 3–45 metres

these communities is still visible.

The path ends in Port Union. Possibly the only union-built town in North America, Port Union was the brainchild of Sir William Coaker. Take time to visit the museum in the former Reid Railway station dating from 1917 and Coaker's bungalow.

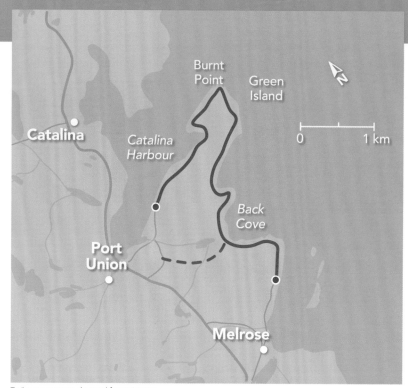

Burnt
Point

Green
Island

Catalina

Catalina
Harbour

0   1 km

Back
Cove

Port
Union

Melrose

Trail maps are **not to be used for navigation.**

Champney's West

This trail starts in Champney's West and leads out to Fox Island, which is not actually an island but joined to Champney's by a stretch of beach. As you enter the community, keep right and look for the parking and trail sign close to the end of the road.

Most of this hike is a pleasant stroll with negligible elevation gain; it leaves the main road through the

community and leads out across the plateau toward Michael's Head and Backside Cove.

Caplin, a major source of food for whales, seals, cod, and seabirds, are plentiful in this area. In late June and early July, large numbers of them "roll" in waves onto the beaches to spawn. People gather the little fish (about 20–25 centimetres in length) to fry, dry for later use, or fertilize their vegetable gardens.

Distance: 3-kilometre loop

Trailhead: Champney's West (48.225975, -53.180871)

Highlights: Headland views, beach

Elev. range: 0–35 metres

The more adventurous will want to clamber to the summit, 35 metres above sea level. From the top are magnificent views in all directions and opportunities for exploration around the promontory. Be careful when climbing up and descending the narrow trail; the ground is uneven and the trail may be overgrown with tall grass and weeds.

After the climb, rest on the beach; it has been a favourite picnic site of local people for many generations. Whales are known to lunge-feed in Robin Hood Bay.

From the beach, several alternative paths link up and rejoin the road. Take the road back to your car or, if you have time, return on the path the way you came.

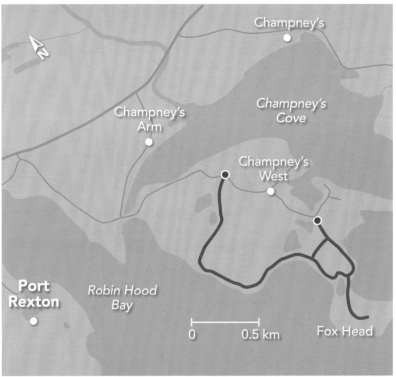

Champney's

Champney's Cove

Champney's Arm

Champney's West

Port Rexton

Robin Hood Bay

0   0.5 km

Fox Head

Trail maps are **not to be used for navigation.**

Trinity East

Skerwink is another name for the shearwater, large seabirds commonly seen during the summer months off the coast of Newfoundland. The trail, which is named for these birds, is the crown jewel of hiking trails on the Bonavista Peninsula. Only 5 kilometres long, it boasts all the features hikers hope for in a coastal hike: sea stacks, cliffs, beaches, grassy headlands, and, from the summit, a panoramic view of the surrounding area.

From the well-marked parking area in Trinity East the trail follows the old railbed to the coast and then the cliff, alternating between tree-sheltered pathways and open headlands. Kittiwakes and cormorants may be seen and, if you are lucky, a bald eagle or two.

Look for the side trail that leads to the lookout at the top of the hill. The summit affords a spectacular view of Trinity Bight and six communities; a picnic table is provided and is an ideal place to have lunch.

Returning to the main path you will soon descend to a long beach called Sam White's Cove; from there, turn right, cross a meadow, and return via a gravel path to the starting point in Trinity East.

Travel and Leisure magazine named the Skerwink Trail one of the top 35 walks in Europe and North America. The trail has received rave reviews in national and international publications and is enjoyed by hundreds of hikers every year.

Distance:
5-kilometre linear trail

Trailhead: Trinity East
(48.224526, -53.202473)

Highlights: Coastal views, seabirds, and icebergs and whales in season

Elev. range: 3–60 metres

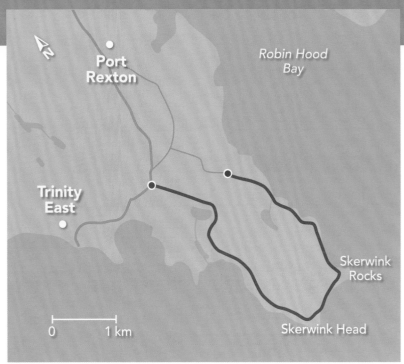

Trail maps are **not to be used for navigation.**

New Bonaventure to British Harbour

This trail begins near New Bonaventure at the *Random Passage* film location. This site attracts thousands of visitors every year, and there is plenty of parking.

This linear hike is 12 kilometres return, but it is possible to avoid backtracking by taking a boat from New Bonaventure to British Harbour. Boat tour operators provide this service during tourist season.

> ★ This trail offers a chance to learn about traditional outport Newfoundland, as does the *Random Passage* site, which depicts what an isolated eighteenth- or nineteenth-century outport would have looked like.

In 2014, only a few summer cabins remained at British Harbour, once a bustling outport of over 200 people. The trail itself begins behind the community, which was resettled in the 1970s.

Distance: 6-kilometre linear trail (12-kilometre return)

Trailheads: New Bonaventure (48.170817, -53.270864); British Harbour (48.154839, -53.300076)

Highlights: Resettled communities

Elev. range: 12–156 metres

The trail climbs steadily out of British Harbour as it leaves the coast, arriving at a bald rocky height of land which provides a view of British Harbour and a panorama of rugged country and ponds. Expect to encounter deadfall trees and muddy sections as this trail has had little maintenance. In a few places extra care is required as the path is steep.

Kerley's Harbour, another resettled outport, is the last point of interest along the trail before arriving at the film set. A road links the site to the town of New Bonaventure about 1 kilometre away.

Old Bonaventure

New Bonaventure

Smith Sound

Wolf Head

British Harbour

0   1 km   2 km

Trail maps are **not to be used for navigation**.

1 King's Cove

The community of King's Cove is often overlooked in favour of some of the more heavily market-ed communities on the Bonavista Peninsula such as Bonavista and Trinity. Don't make this mistake—it is a gem. This community on the western side of the peninsula is picturesque and the trail to its lighthouse an easy and rewarding hike.

The elegant spire of Saints Peter and Paul Catholic Church is easy to spot and hikers should park near the church. The trail runs parallel to Blackhead Bay in the direction of the lighthouse about 1 kilome-tre away.

From the lighthouse, take the extended loop that goes by way of Fish Point Lookout and Brook Point Lookout. The sediments that are exposed on the cliff face at Brook Point are composed of 500-million-year-old Cambrian rock. The distinct colour variation is the first feature that catches your eye. The thick layers that dip sharply to the water's edge consist of red sandstones and conglomer-ates from the Crown Hill geologi-

cal formation. The green and grey sandstone and siltstone contain copper.

The trail passes Round Pond Steady and Round Pond before traversing Pat Murphy's Meadow, made famous in "When I Mowed Pat Murphy's Meadow," the song written in the 1930s by King's Cove native J.M. Devine.

Trail maps are not to be used for navigation.

King's Cove Lighthouse, shipped in sections from Birmingham, England, and assembled on-site in King's Cove in 1893, is an imposing structure. It was a manned lighthouse until 2000, when it was automated.

Distance: 3.5 kilometres

Trailheads: Saints Peter and Paul Catholic Church, King's Cove (48.341052, -53.200128)

Highlights: Church, lighthouse, Brook Point

Elev. range: 0–63 metres

These hikes are located in the area referred to in the delightful Newfoundland folk song "All around the Circle" (also known as "I'se the B'y"). Tourism in this area has grown in recent years, and many accommodations and amenities are readily available for hikers. The rich local history, combined with the hospitality and services, breathtaking scenery, and hiking experiences, will make you want to return to this region again and again.

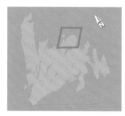

The Road to the Shore is a loop of highway beginning at Gambo, travelling along the northeast coast, and returning to the Trans-Canada Highway at the airport town of Gander. Gambo is famous as the birthplace of Joseph Smallwood, Newfoundland and Labrador's first premier. Farther along route 320, near Hare Bay, is the Dover Fault, where continents collided and formed the island of Newfoundland 410 million years ago. The coastal towns of Greenspond, Badger's Quay, Wesleyville, Newtown, and Musgrave Harbour are picturesque and rich in history. The long sandy beaches of Cape Freels and Lumsden offer the opportunity to explore and wander freely along this strikingly beautiful coast.

Fogo Island sits at the extreme edge of Notre Dame Bay. It is separated from the Newfoundland mainland by Hamilton Sound and 16 kilometres of ocean.

The name *Fogo* may have evolved from the Portuguese word for fire, *fuego*, perhaps referring to the forest fires that were seen regularly in the area. Portugal was one of the many European nations that fished these rich coastal waters. Fogo Island has a dramatic landscape: the northern part is an undulating plain of exposed bedrock, lichen, and treeless bogs; the southern shore is blanketed by tangled forest and boggy wetlands. Note of caution: Many of the traditional trails on the island continue beyond the descriptions we give here. Be prepared with a topographical map of the area if you wish to attempt longer hikes on unmarked trails.

Change Islands consists of three islands; the two larger islands are inhabited and connected by a causeway. Change Islands is located in Notre Dame Bay between Twillingate and

Fogo. One story suggests that the name originated because ships "going down the Labrador" to fish or to hunt seals changed crews there. Another claims that the name was given because the inhabitants changed islands during the year, remaining on the north island for the summer fishing season and moving south to be closer to sources of wood for the winter months.

Twillingate's earliest European presence was French fishers who visited the area each summer between 1650 and 1690 and named the island Toulinquet for its likeness to a group of islands located off Brest, France. English settlers (also known as "livyers"), unfamiliar with the French language, changed the name of the island to Twillingate. Over the next centuries, Twillingate, with its rich fishing grounds and safe harbour, developed into one of Newfoundland's most prosperous ports. Merchants bought fish to sell in Spain and Portugal and provided fishers with salt and other supplies—money rarely changed hands. Today Twillingate prospers as a tourism destination.

Road to the Shore

53. Middle Brook River Trail
54. Greenspond Island Trail
55. Cape Island Walking Trail

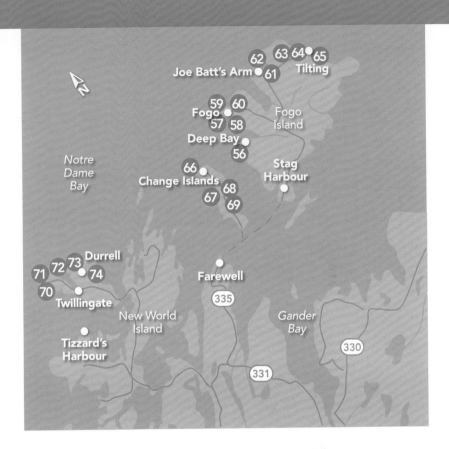

Fogo Island

56. Deep Bay
57. Waterman's Brook Trail
58. Brimstone Head Trail
59. Fogo Head Trail
60. Lion's Den Trail
61. Shoal Bay Trail
62. Great Auk Trail
63. Turpin's Trail West
64. Turpin's Trail East
65. Oliver's Cove Footpath

Change Islands

66. Squid Jigger Trail
67. Shoreline Path
68. Salt Water Pond Loop
69. Indian Lookout

Twillingate

70. Lower Head Loop
71. Sleepy Cove Trail
72. French Beach to Spiller's Cove Trail
73. Spiller's Cove to Codjack's Cove Trail
74. Lower Little Harbour Trail

1

Gambo

The Middle Brook River Trail in the David Smallwood Park on the northern outskirts of Gambo at Middle Cove is a loop path and can be started on either side of the river.

This is a well-maintained path with many interesting storyboards about the natural history and early habitation of the area.

It is not unusual to encounter anglers along the banks of this beautiful salmon river with its many rattles and waterfalls. At the farthest point upstream, you'll find a side

trail leading to a fish ladder which enables salmon to circumvent the falls. If you look down through the metal grate, it is sometimes possible to see salmon as they swim upstream—some seem to prefer to leap up the falls without the help of a ladder! Benches offer perfect viewing sites.

Another side trail, on the north side of the river, is called Madeline's Path. Madeline was a member of a Mik'maq band that lived in the area, and the path leads to a 200-year-old cemetery.

The entire trail offers a stroll more than a hike, but it is enjoyable and suitable for all ages. As the trail hugs the riverbanks, there is little elevation change but plenty of scenic picnic opportunities.

Distance: 3-kilometre loop trail

Trailhead: David Smallwood Park (48.482118, -54.123148)

Highlights: River, waterfall, salmon ladder

Elev. range: 1–6 metres

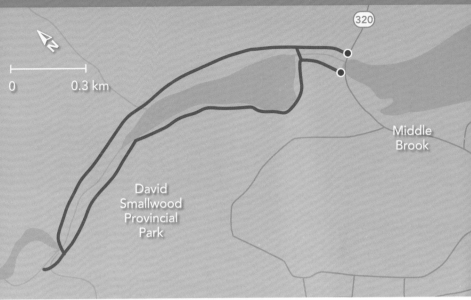

320

Middle
Brook

David
Smallwood
Provincial
Park

0   0.3 km

Trail maps are **not to be used for navigation.**

Greenspond

Settlers from England's West Country established a community on Greenspond Island in 1697, making it one of the oldest continuously inhabited settlements in Newfoundland. Over the centuries Greenspond has played a vital role in the cod fishery and the seal hunt. With the establishment of a customs house in 1838, it became known as the "capital of the north."

The construction of a causeway between Greenspond Island and the mainland in the 1980s has made this little gem of an island easily accessible to visitors. Signs on the main road through the community make it easy to find the trailhead for the Greenspond Island Trail, a path which hugs the coastline around most of the island.

This is an easy hike with low-lying coastal features and no steep sections. The undulating topography has been made even more pleasant to manoeuvre by long sections of substantial boardwalk and stairway. The community takes pride in the trail and a sign asks

hikers to report any areas in need of repairs.

Signs along the route identify points of interest. At Cannister Cove, hikers can turn inland to take a shortcut back to Main Road or continue along the shore to the end of the trail. The walk back through the community goes past the historic courthouse built in 1899, once the centre for justice for the entire northeast coast of Newfoundland.

Distance: 3.5-kilometre loop

Trailhead: End of Main Road, Greenspond (49.041594, -53.335422)

Highlights: Stark, treeless topography; whale viewing; seabirds; berries in season

Elev. range: 3–50 metres

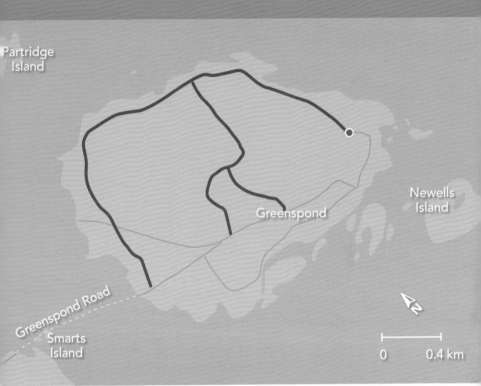

Partridge
Island

Greenspond

Newells
Island

Greenspond Road

Smarts
Island

0   0.4 km

N

Trail maps are **not to be used for navigation.**

Cape Freels

Anyone who has read the novel *Random Passage*, by Bernice Morgan, will know that Cape Island was the home of the Vincents and the Andrews, the principal families in the book. The Cape Island Walking Trail takes hikers out to the place where the novel is set and these families lived.

From Route 330, take the Cape Freels Road and look for the sign indicating the trailhead for the Cape Island Walking Trail. Take the

 Although the novel *Random Passage* was set on the shores of Cape Freels, the TV miniseries was filmed in New Bonaventure on the Bonavista Peninsula (see British Harbour Trail, hike 51).

Distance: 6-kilometre return

Trailhead: Cape Freels Road
(49.150748, -53.291242)

Highlights: Beach, cemetery, site of old settlement

Elev. range: 0–5 metres

ATV track over a small footbridge and then turn left. A path will bring you to the shoreline, where a beautiful broad sandy beach seems to stretch on forever. Turn right and walk along the beach. Look for shorebirds such as yellowlegs as you head south.

Nestled among large outcrops of smooth granite slabs at the end of the beach is a small graveyard with the headstones of members of the families who lived, toiled, and died here before the community was resettled in 1950. The location of the former settlement is nearby, but all that is left is the remains of a root cellar.

You will hardly get higher than a few metres above sea level on this hike; the shore is very low-lying—unlike most of Newfoundland's topography—but it is a starkly beautiful coastline.

Hikers have the option of taking the track or the beach back to the trailhead.

Middle Bill Cove

Cape Freels South

Cape Cove

330

0   2 km

Trail maps are **not to be used for navigation.**

Deep Bay

This gem of a trail is short and steep and an artist's haven. Situated within the town of Deep Bay, the trail traces a route almost due south of the starting point. In Deep Bay, park by the Shorefast House, an artist's residence on the south side of the road about halfway through town.

The hike begins with a steep climb up a wooden staircase just behind the Shorefast House. The subarctic vegetation changes noticeably as you near the top of the climb, becoming more stunted with elevation.

The trail levels out at the top, revealing a spectacular view of Brimstone Head to the north. Ground cover is sparse; harsh wind, salt spray, and thin soil deter the growth of vegetation.

The Bridge Studio is your reward for reaching the top. This is one of four artists' studios built by the Shorefast Foundation on Fogo Island. On closer inspection you will not question the positioning of the structure. One end of the building faces a small pond, providing

views of nature that would inspire anyone.

This is another one of those places where you can explore, berry pick, and relax for hours. Just remember to take a map and compass and perhaps a guide, if you want to ramble off-trail.

Distance: 0.6-kilometre linear trail (1.2-kilometre return)

Trailhead: Shorefast House (49.401786, -54.174097)

Highlights: View of Brimstone Head, orchids, berries, geology, Bridge Studio

Elev. range: 10–250 metres

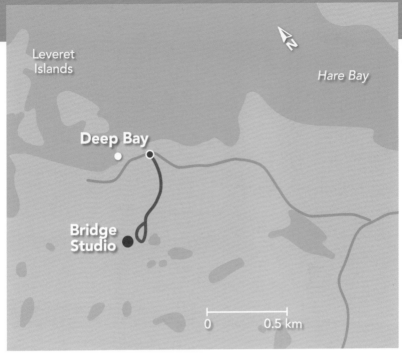

Leveret
Islands

Hare Bay

Deep Bay

Bridge
Studio

0   0.5 km

Trail maps are **not to be used for navigation.**

Town of Fogo

This inland trail weaves through boreal forest, barrens, and pond-sides and features an abundance of wildflowers. Wild berries are plentiful in season.

The trailhead is located in a large firewood storage area on the west side of the road just before you enter the town of Fogo. The well-marked trail consists of a board-walk and steps which protect the natural vegetation.

The views of the ocean are spec-tacular. According to local history, men going to the lumber woods on the mainland or sealers head-ing to the icefields off Labrador

Distance: 4-kilometre linear trail (8-kilometre return)

Trailhead: Main road before entering the town of Fogo (49.424260, -54.162847)

Highlights: Views from Wood-peck Hill Lookout, vegetation

Elev. range: 10–45 metres

walked though this area to catch their ships. The trail ends at Water-man's Brook Bridge.

The view from the platform at Woodpeck Hill Lookout to the north to Brimstone Head in the town of Fogo demands a panora-ma lens.

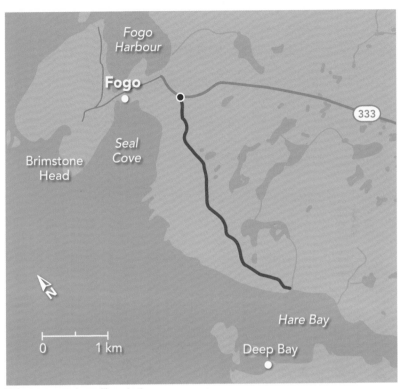

Trail maps are **not to be used for navigation.**

Town of Fogo

The town of Fogo has three trails listed which can be walked as one linear hike, but for the sake of clarity we refer to them as two trails (Brimstone Head Trail and Fogo Head Trail); the third (not described in this book) is the link between the two.

The hike to the top of Brimstone Head is not to be missed: If the steep climb on the wooden staircase doesn't take your breath away, the 360-degree view from the top certainly will. On a windy day fasten any headgear on tightly.

The geology of the area near the town of Fogo is known to be volcanic. The geologic process for the formation of Brimstone Head is more exactly described as *ignimbrite* (from the Latin *igni-* [fire] and *imbri-* [rain]).

Brimstone Head can also boast being one of the four corners of the earth, according to the Flat Earth Society.

★ The Flat Earth model suggests that the earth's shape is a plane or disk. Many ancient cultures had conceptions of a flat earth, including Greece until the fifth century BC, India until 500 BC, and China until the 17th century. The Flat Earth Society has designated the four corners of the earth as Papua New Guinea, the Bermuda Triangle, Fogo, and Hydra (Greece).

Distance:
1.9-kilometre linear trail

Trailhead: Near campground/ baseball diamond in the town of Fogo (49.425590, -54.173976)

Highlights: View from the top, one of four corners of the earth, ancient volcano

Elev. range: 20–85 metres

Western Island

Middle Rock

Garrison Point

Fogo Head Trail

Fogo Harbour

Little Harbour

Fogo

333

Pound Rocks

Banks Cove

Seal Cove

Brimstone Head Trail

Brimstone Head

0   0.5 km

Town of Fogo

This trail can be hiked as a stand-alone linear trail or connected to make a loop trail to include the hike to Brimstone Head and back to Garrison Point.

By the parking area at the beginning of the trail a large viewing platform displays interpretative panels explaining the history of Fogo. Six large cannons serve as reminders of military challenges in the past.

The spectacular hike includes glacial and volcanic features. Wooden staircases, built to withstand the harsh treatment by Mother Nature in this part of the globe, make it easy to walk over the rugged terrain. Several climbs along the trail are steep and seemingly endless, but viewing platforms along the way are well placed so you can catch your breath and relax. The top of Fogo Head is a magical place to take in a glorious sunset if conditions allow.

At Garrison Point Battery, six cannons (9-pounders) were installed in 1771 as a defense against American and French privateers.

Distance:
5-kilometre linear trail

Trailhead: The Battery above Garrison Point, town of Fogo (49.432962, -54.165431)

Highlights: View to Brimstone Head, large cannons at Garrison Point Battery, glacial features

Elev. range: 25–103 metres

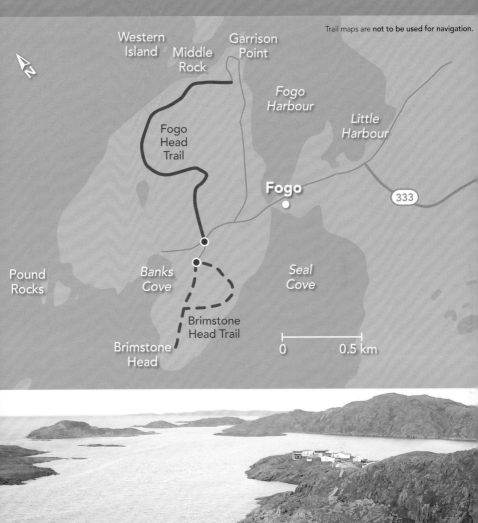

Trail maps are **not to be used for navigation**.

Western
Island
Middle
Rock
Garrison
Point

Fogo
Harbour

Little
Harbour

Fogo
Head
Trail

Fogo

333

Pound
Rocks

Banks
Cove

Seal
Cove

Brimstone
Head Trail

Brimstone
Head

0   0.5 km

Town of Fogo

Lion's Den Trail is one of the flagship trails of Fogo Island. The trailhead is located beside the Marconi Wireless Relay Site and Interpretation Centre on the east side of the town of Fogo. This Marconi site was an important feature of this remote coast from 1912 until newer technology in 1933 made it obsolete. The building provides a view of Fogo Harbour.

The trail is well-marked. Begin by heading northeast from the parking lot. As you crest the first hill, you will catch a breathtaking view of the protected little inlet called the Lion's Den. Stories about how the inlet got its name vary, but you can imagine the name could have originated from the fiercely roaring seas as fishers and explorers navigated into what must have seemed like a lion's maw.

An interpretative panel near sea level in the Lion's Den indicates that the area was first settled in 1836 by fishers from Conception Bay looking for better fishing grounds. Wild daffodils and other once-cultivated flowers are the only reminders of the inhabitants that lived there until the late 1890s.

The hike is superb, offering views to the North Atlantic and, in season, opportunities for iceberg viewing and whale spotting.

 Seeds from cultivated plants, not native to the province, were brought over to the new world inadvertently in or stuck to packing material or ballast. Material such as sods and straw were common packing, and stone was used for ballast. Some of the plants, including daffodils along the Lion's Den Trail and mallow on parts of the East Coast Trail, flourished and adapted to their harsh new environment, and now grow wild.

Distance:
5.4-kilometre loop

Trailhead: Marconi Site
(49.431681, -54.154300)

Highlights: Resettled community, storyboards, Marconi Site

Elev. range: 0–90 metres

Lion's
Den Point

Uncle
Andys
Island

*Lion's Den
Cove*

Light
House
Island

Simms
Island

arnes
land

0   0.5 km

*Fogo
Harbour*

*Freemans
Pond*

ogo
ead

1 ## Joe Batt's Arm

The trail to Shoal Bay begins at the side of the road about halfway between Joe Batt's Arm and the town of Fogo. It is essentially a long narrow boardwalk leading to Tower Studio, one of four architecturally designed artists' studios on Fogo Island.

Walking across a nearly treeless barren with Shoal Bay in the distance, it is impossible not to focus on the intriguingly shaped structure at the end of the boardwalk. As the name suggests, it is a tower—and yet its shape is constantly changing as your angle of view shifts. It is also important to glance down as you walk toward the studio to appreciate the variety of mosses, grasses, and bushes that cling to the rocks and peat bog.

Observe the studio from all angles: It looks solid as a rock from one side and then almost ready to topple over from another. It is a captivating design and, like all the studios, relies on solar panels and wood for electricity and heat.

Distance: 1-kilometre linear trail (2-kilometre return)

Trailhead: Between Fogo and Joe Batt's Arm (49.402936, -54.122445)

Highlights: Shoal Bay, Tower Studio

Elev. range: Minimal

★ The artists' studios and Fogo Island Inn were designed by Todd Saunders, a Newfoundland-born architect now based in Norway. The studios and the inn, all set on sparse landscape far from any other man-made objects, appear as if they have been dropped from outer space. From a distance they look like pieces of sculpture rather than functional buildings. Closer inspection reveals, however, that they have been erected not only with an eye to aesthetics but also with concern for the environment: they have wood-burning stoves for heat, solar panels for electricity, and compost toilets. Natural materials, locally sourced where possible, have been used throughout.

Tower Studio

Shoal Bay

To Joe Batt's Arm

334

0   0.5 km

Trail maps are **not to be used for navigation.**

Joe Batt's Arm

This trail, which starts at Etheridges Point Community Park on the east side in the bay of the community of Joe Batt's Arm, runs almost directly true north along the coast.

Fogo Island Inn can be seen on the west side of the bay. This

 The great auk was found widely in northern habitats, including Newfoundland, Iceland, Greenland, the Faroe Islands, United Kingdom, and Norway. The species became extinct in the 1850s because of over-hunting by sailors and fishers; great auks, which did not fly, made easy prey. A great auk was approximately 70 centimetres in length and weighed 5 kilograms.

Distance: 2.7-kilometre linear trail (5.4-kilometre return)

Trailhead: Etheridges Point (49.435667, -54.092831)

Highlights: Long Studio, Great Auk sculpture, migratory bird sightings

Elev. range: 0–10 metres

modern edifice has been designed to conjure the idea of a traditional fishing store perched on stilts extending toward the water.

Farther along the trail is Long Studio, another of the Shorefast Foundation's artists' studios. This geometric structure seems as if it was simply dropped into place without disturbing the surrounding natural backdrop. You can arrange ahead of time to visit the resident artist or simply walk around the building and admire its architecture on your way by.

Along this well-defined trail are terrific ocean views, community gardens, picnic spots, and rest places; wildflowers are abundant. Because of its location in the North Atlantic, this area is also a haven to migrating birds, including whimbrels.

At the end of this trail, the hiker is rewarded with the sight of a 2-metre-tall bronze sculpture of a great auk by Todd McGrain, perched upright and anchored in concrete on a massive sloping rock outcrop.

Trail maps are **not to be used for navigation.**

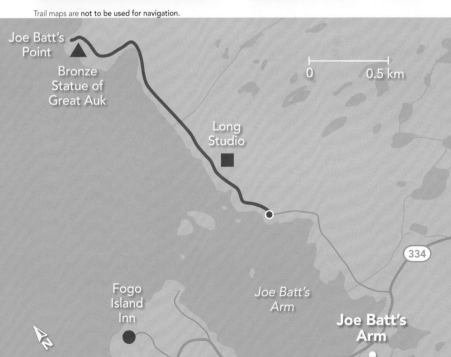

Tilting

Turpin's Trail has been divided, in this book, into two experiences— Turpin's Trail West and Turpin's Trail East—as they are very different and each can be a day hike. Ample parking for Turpin's Trail West can be found on Farm Road. Unlike many of the other trails on Fogo Island, this one begins in a densely wooded area and transitions through several distinct vegetation zones. Informative storyboards along the trail present information about the vegetation and habitats you'll see along the route.

The boreal forest is the first zone encountered; this part of the island is in the North Shore Forest Ecoregion. Its climate has the warmest summers of any coastal region of the province, and the forest is dominated by black spruce and balsam fir. The trail progresses through a fen landscape, then opens into a coastal landscape.

Stones mark this low coastal part of the trail. An upturned dory and a few lobster pots have rotted and bleached in the salty spray and constant winds off the North Atlantic. At Seal Cove, an interpre-

 Fens versus Bogs
Because fens, wetlands that form in hollows in the landscape, are neutral in acidity, they provide an area of high productivity and greater variety of plants and animals. Bogs are dominated by sphagnum moss, which is acidic and not hospitable to a wide variety of vegetation.

tative panel describes the features of rocky shores. Explore the lovely little beach and then cool your feet in the crystal-clear water.

The trail continues in a loop back to the parking area and includes a stunning sandy beach at Sandy Cove. The history of the area is full of stories of confrontation between the local Aboriginal inhabitants, the Beothuks, and the early European settlers. The namesake of this trail, Michael Turpin, fought a battle in 1809 which cost him his head.

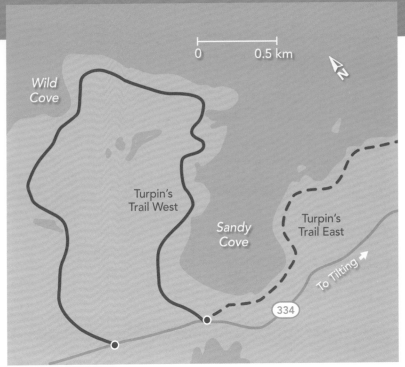

Trail maps are not to be used for navigation.

Distance: 3.1-kilometre loop

Trailhead: Farm Road parking area west of Sandy Cove Beach (49.423220, -54.032646)

Highlights: Transition of vegetation and landscapes

Elev. range: 0–35 metres

Tilting

The scenic town of Tilting is a photographer's paradise; be sure to allow time to stroll through the town. The homes, outbuildings, and fishing premises are generally well-preserved, teeming with history of a seafaring folk.

Turpin's Trail East starts at the award-winning Lane House Museum, the only house in Tilting with a spiral staircase. The original owner, Augie Mac, a barrel maker by trade, knew the space-saving function of a spiral design.

The trail heads in a northeast direction, over gently undulating terrain, and is clearly marked. Perched on the shoreline close to the start of the trail you will see Squish Studio, a white box-shaped structure hugging the rugged rocks. This is the fourth of the four artists' studios created by the Shorefast Foundation on the island (see hikes 46, 51, and 52 for the others).

The trail meanders past fenced vegetable gardens, sheep, abandoned lobster pots, and spectacular sea views. Seabirds are plentiful; yellow legs are a common sight on the beach at Sandy Cove. Whales and icebergs are familiar sights from June to late August.

As you round the last headland, the view opens up to Sandy Cove Beach, a beautiful white sandy expanse that slopes gently into the ocean.

 Greater Yellow Legs, *Tringa melanoleuca*, is a medium-sized shorebird, approximately 35 centimetres in height, seen in Atlantic Canada. Its habitat includes bogs, alluvial wetlands, fens, and beaver ponds. The bird can be identified by its call, a quick whistled series of three times *tew-tew-tew*.

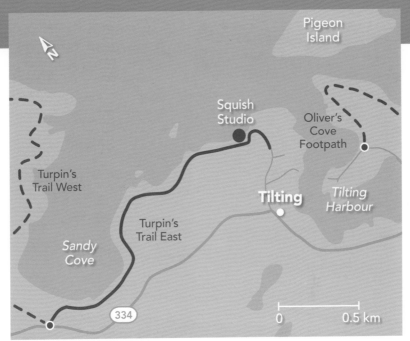

Trail maps are **not to be used for navigation.**

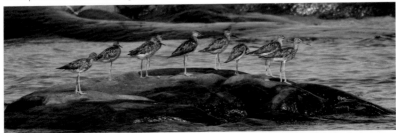

Distance:
4.6-kilometre linear trail

Trailhead:
Lane House Museum
(49.422828, -54.035097)

Highlights: Historic town
of Tilting, coastal features,
seabirds, vegetable gardens,
Squish Studio, sandy beach

Elev. range: 0–30 metres

1 Tilting

The painted fishing sheds perched on islands of granite slabs in the harbour of Tilting are memorable images. It is believed that the name of the community stems from the term "tilt," a flimsy cabin built by migratory fishermen. The architecture of 21st-century Tilting no longer includes "tilts," but it has been studied and profiled in a book of the same name by the architect Robert Mellin.

This loop trail starts on the east side of Tilting Harbour. At the end of Harbour Road, head east and follow a path around to Oliver's Cove, which can include scrambling over and between huge beach rocks. The Devil's Chair is one such massive block of granite in which erosion has created a perfect perch to sit on. For gentler footing, remain on the trail in the grassy meadow.

Ocean views, and whale and iceberg viewing in season, are fabulous on this shore. Along the trail an array of wildflowers and plants, including oyster grass, add colour to your journey. At the south end of the trail, large community gardens slope to the sea. Root cellars, in particular cabbage cellars, are detailed on the storyboards.

 Root cellars were often built into the earth and covered with layers of sod. Cabbage cellars, however, were constructed a little differently, as cabbages need a drier storage. Cabbage cellars were often made from an overturned punt (a small open boat) buried in a well-drained area, with the entrance at the rear of the punt. Cabbages, with their roots still intact, were often hung from the roof (the floor of the punt) rather than on the ground, where wet rot could set in.

Distance:
4.5-kilometre loop

Trailhead:
East side of the harbour in Tilting (49.422871, -50.033062)

Highlights: Geology, coastal features, wildflowers, gardens, root cellars

Elev. range: 0–10 metres

Pigeon
Island

Oliver's
Cove Footpath

urpin's
ail East

Tilting

334

*Tilting
Harbour*

*Oliver's
Cove*

0   0.5 km

Trail maps are **not** to be used for navigation.

Change Islands

This 3-kilometre linear trail takes you along the northernmost shoreline of Change Islands. Signs are plentiful along the length of the hike, which can easily be made into a loop by adding the delightful walk along the main road of this tiny community back to the beginning.

The terrain varies from dry rocky lookouts to spongy bog to meadowscapes with an abundance of wildflowers in summer, including a sea of blue when blue flag irises are in bloom. Headstones in the graveyard beside along the path reveal surnames common to the island.

 The waters near this trail are said to be the location that inspired the famous Newfoundland folk song "Squid Jiggin' Ground," written by native son A.R. Scammell at the age of 15. Released in 1943, this lively song with irreverent lyrics is still heard at folk-music events around the province.

The trail is gently undulating for the most part, with sections of boardwalk, but be careful on the stairs on steeper sections. The shoreline is pocked with small coves of crystal-clear shallow water ideal for wading or exploring by kayak.

Distance: 3-kilometre linear trail (6.5 kilometres if you make it a loop hike by walking back on the road)

Trailheads:
East side of the North Island (49.404588, -54.235691); west side of the North Island (49.404726, -54.252478)

Highlights:
Wildflowers, ocean views

Elev. range: 0–21 metres

The trail is perfect for iceberg viewing if you are there when these icy behemoths float by, usually between May and August. The other giants which can be viewed on this hike are whales. On a clear day you can also see one of the four corners of the earth, according to the Flat Earth Society, at Brimstone Head (see hike 48) on neighbouring Fogo Island.

Trail maps are **not to be used for navigation.**

Change Islands

This delightfully diverse path takes you through so many landscapes that it makes the name of the trail rather deceiving. The Shoreline Path is actually a series of traditional trails linked along the west side of the island approximately parallel to the main highway.

There are several entrances and exits to this 5-kilometre linear trail. Like all of the trails on the island, the joy of walking is not immediately obvious from the trailheads, but

the magic begins once you have left the view of the road behind.

At the Birch Cove entrance you will walk into thick birch woodland along a well-trodden path. You would never guess you are on a shoreline path. Signs of beaver activity are obvious: large logs strewn around bear the characteristic chatter marks from *Castor canadensis*'s long front teeth. About 10 minutes in, you'll see meadows through the trees, and then the beach at Birch Cove. You may see up to a dozen Newfoundland Ponies grazing in a large fenced paddock. Change Islands boasts a state-of-the-art pony refuge (www. nlponysanctuary.com), completed in 2015. After hiking the trails, drop in to see the animals in their new digs. Tell Netta we sent you!

Remarkable geological structures, like the almost vertical sedimentary

 The Newfoundland Pony is native to Newfoundland with ancestors, like many of the human inhabitants of Newfoundland, from the British Isles. These ponies traditionally ploughed gardens, carried kelp from the beaches, and hauled wood for the long Newfoundland winters. Their numbers in 2016 are not high. To protect against their extinction, the Newfoundland government has given them a designation of Heritage Animal; despite that effort, they are still considered an endangered species. Their average lifespan is 25 to 30 years.

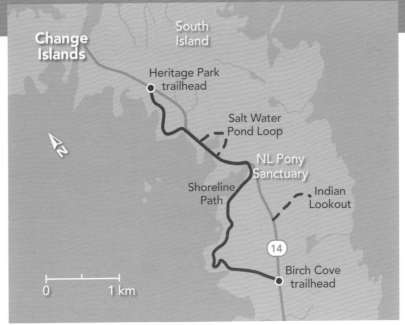

Trail maps are **not to be used for navigation**.

layers which were initially deposited horizontally, can be seen along the trail. The beach, strewn with treasures the sea heaved upon it, is a beachcomber's paradise. Picnic spots abound.

The path weaves in and out along the shoreline, sometimes connecting with the road, and ends at Heritage Park. Climb the Bird Gaze Lookout for a full view of the coast.

Distance:
6.3-kilometre linear trail

Trailheads:
Birch Cove (49.375603, -54.235550); Heritage Park (49.392432, -54.235313)

Highlights: Beaver, Newfoundland Ponies, geology, beachcombing, Bird Gaze Lookout

Elev. range: 10–30 metres

Change Islands

An easy walk around this little pond is a treat for any nature lover. The trail runs close to a main highway, which may cause some to avoid it—however, the highway or main road running north-south on Change Islands is not busy by any stretch of the imagination and will not cloud your enjoyment of the walk.

There is only one parking area, which is easy to find, by the only body of water on the east (right) side of the main road heading north from the ferry. It is about 2 kilometres south of the causeway-bridge that links the north and south islands.

This is an exceptional area for nature viewing, particularly birds, from one of the many natural "blinds" or shel-

 This salt water inlet is a birder's haven.

Distance:
1.5-kilometre loop

Trailhead: Parking lot at Salt Water Pond (49.390269, -54.235321)

Highlights:
Birds, ducks, wildflowers

Elev. range: Gently undulating

tered viewing spots along the trail. The boardwalk and gently undulating terrain are easy on the hiker's feet and legs.

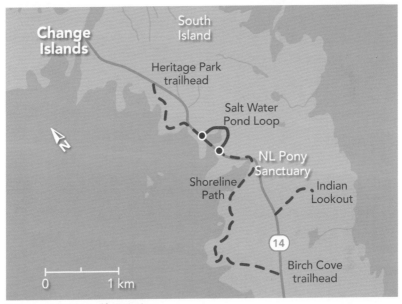

Change Islands

South Island

Heritage Park trailhead

Salt Water Pond Loop

NL Pony Sanctuary

Shoreline Path

Indian Lookout

14

Birch Cove trailhead

0   1 km

Trail maps are **not to be used for navigation.**

Change Islands

Along this coast, with its hundreds of small islands, lookout trails are common. But reaching the top of any one of them never fails to give the hiker a thrill of achievement. This trail starts at a most unlikely spot along the main road running north-south along the spine of Change Islands.

The sign is hidden slightly; it is located in a large parking lot for firewood storage. On the right side of the lot a sign points to the Indian Lookout trail.

This is a linear trail with considerable elevation change; it is a lookout trail, after all! The trail is a pleasant hike through mixed woodland, with sets of stairs that take hikers to the highest point on the island.

The view of the coastline far below is breathtaking. Fogo Island is directly to the east.

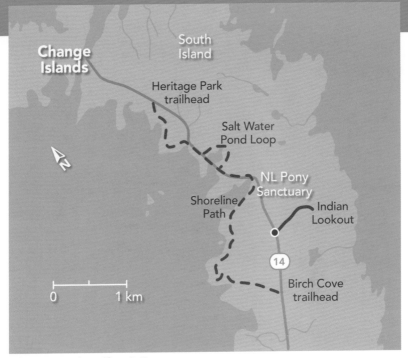

Change Islands

South Island

Heritage Park trailhead

Salt Water Pond Loop

NL Pony Sanctuary

Shoreline Path

Indian Lookout

 14

Birch Cove trailhead

0   1 km

Trail maps are **not to be used for navigation.**

INDIAN LOOKOUT

★ The origins of the trail's name are unclear. Was it named for Indians looking out for European settlers, or settlers looking out for Indians?

Distance: 1-kilometre linear trail (2-kilometre return)

Trailhead: Wood storage depot on east side of main highway (49.380618, -54.234335)

Highlights: Woodland, views from lookout, highest point of Change Islands

Elev. range: 0–78 metres

Crow Head

This trail is one of several hikes in the Crow Head area of Twillingate (see hike 61). Although the hikes can be linked for a day of hiking, they deserve individual descriptions.

The hike to Lower Head begins at the parking lot of Sea Breeze Park. The trail begins with a climb up some fairly substantial wooden steps through an area of black spruce.

The landscape is varied; hiking poles will help navigate the undulations in the path. Wildflowers grow abundantly along the trail, but the view from the top is the most impressive

Distance: 3-kilometre loop

Trailhead: Sea Breeze Park (49.405982, -54.482127)

Highlights: Rugged cliffs, ocean views, whales, icebergs

Elev. range: 5–45 metres

feature of this hike. The ocean around the base of the cliffs is aqua and, in season, home to whales and icebergs.

The loop back to the beginning starts with a steep scramble from the top and then evens to a much-used trail through low bush.

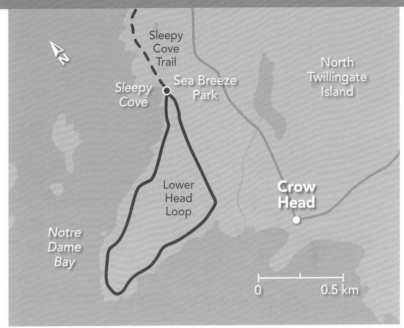

Sleepy
Cove
Trail

Sleepy
Cove

Sea Breeze
Park

North
Twillingate
Island

Lower
Head
Loop

Crow
Head

Notre
Dame
Bay

0   0.5 km

Trail maps are **not to be used for navigation.**

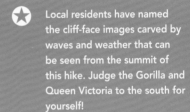

Local residents have named the cliff-face images carved by waves and weather that can be seen from the summit of this hike. Judge the Gorilla and Queen Victoria to the south for yourself!

Crow Head

This is a dramatic linear coastal trail. The trailhead, depending on an up- or downhill hiking preference, can be accessed from near sea level in Sleepy Cove or at a 100-metre elevation at the west side of the parking lot of Long Point Lighthouse.

 Local history claims that, at Nanny's Hole, grazing nanny goats fell into crevasses and holes near the rugged coastline and the holes have been named for these wandering goats.

From the platform at Long Point, the view of the sea is breathtaking. At any time of year the sight and sound of the roaring waves at the base of rugged sheer cliff faces are stunning. During the summer months, from the viewing platform, you can see whales approaching close enough to be clearly visible though the crystal-clear water. From June to August icebergs are the area's other star attractions.

 Sleepy Cove has remnants of a copper mining operation run by Obediah Hodder of Pennsylvania from 1906 to 1917.

From the parking lot, the trail descends via a series of steep steps. At the bottom a signpost offers a choice of trails. One leads to a viewpoint called Nanny's Hole to the right and Sleepy Cove to the left. Sea stacks just offshore offer photo opportunities. In summer the area is busy with tourists taking in whale-watching and iceberg tours.

Distance: 2-kilometre linear trail (4-kilometre return)

Trailheads: Sea Breeze Park (49.405982, -54.482127); Long Point Lighthouse (49.411393, -54.480337)

Highlights: Rugged coastline, sea stacks, copper mine remnants, lighthouse

Elev. range: 25–100 metres

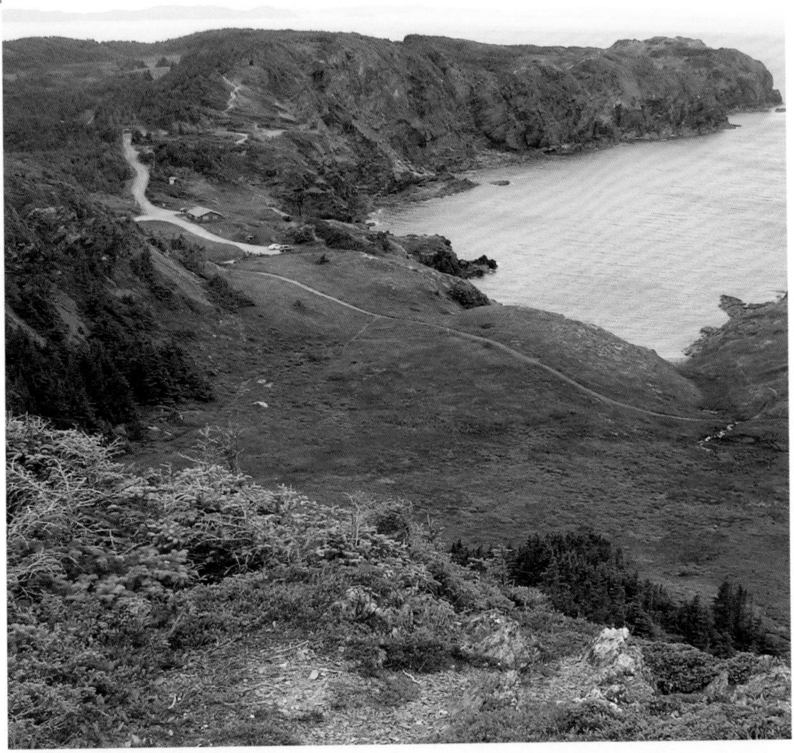

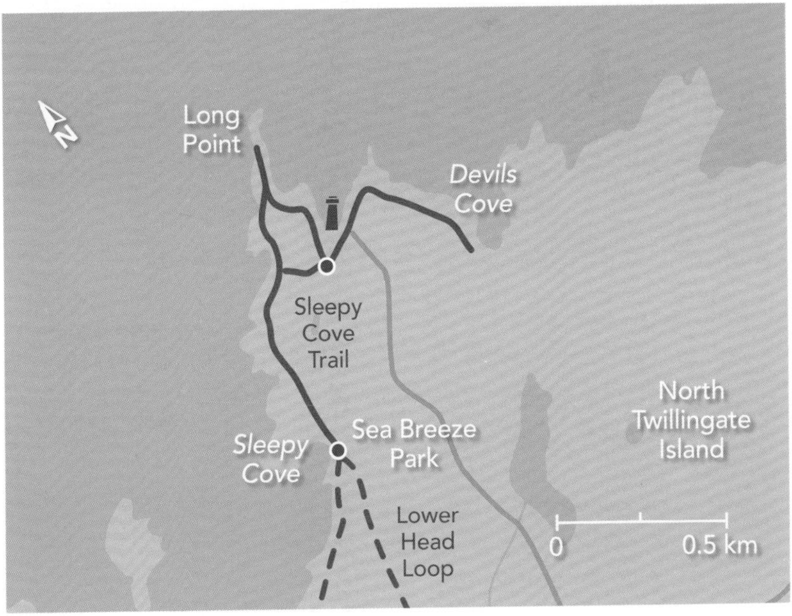

Long Point
Devils Cove
Sleepy Cove Trail
Sleepy Cove
Sea Breeze Park
Lower Head Loop
North Twillingate Island
0
0.5 km

Trail maps are **not to be used for navigation.**

Durrell

The trailhead is located at the end of the road on the south side of Durrell's Arm near Blow Me Down Lane. The first view you'll catch along this trail is of French Beach, a stunning rocky beach of mostly pink granite pebbles. This trail has several loops to explore, depending on how much time you have to wander.

The terrain varies from sea level to 70 metres. Rugged coastal features include sea stacks, caves, and rock formations, some of which the local residents have named, including Cobra, Camel, and Indian. Vegetation varies from low shrubs on the north side of the trail to dense spruce woodland to beach and then bogland on the path from Spiller's Cove back to the start of the trail.

At Spiller's Cove, look for the enormous osprey nest, located safely on a sea stack or spiller—in early summer, you may even see chicks.

The wide beach is ideal for beachcombing or relaxing. From the beach the trail turns inland to the trailhead, or hikers may continue on to Codjack's Cove.

Offshore rocks at three different Spillars (Spillers) Coves around the province feature tall, thin, and tapered formations known as sea stacks. These place names may have derived from the term "spiller" or "spill," a small cylinder on which yarn was wound (according to the *Dictionary of Newfoundland English*), or a peg or pin for plugging a hole (*Merriam-Webster Dictionary*). Both items would have been familiar to early European sailors, who may have identified the similarities in the features and named the locations to reflect that.

Distance: 5–7-kilometre loop

Trailhead: Blow Me Down Lane (49.400770, -54.433539)

Highlights: Rugged coastline, sea stacks

Elev. range: 0–85 metres

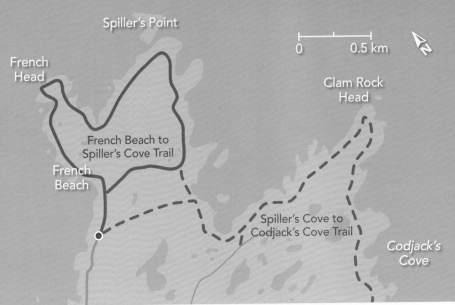

Spiller's Point

French Head

French Beach to Spiller's Cove Trail

French Beach

0   0.5 km

Clam Rock Head

Spiller's Cove to Codjack's Cove Trail

Codjack's Cove

Durrell

This trail starts in the community of Durrell near the head of the bay called Durrell's Arm. Head east at the end of Horwood Lane; trail signs in the community are clear.

This loop hike leads to Codjack's Cove and its coastal views. Sea stacks, caves, and rugged cliffs make it a photographer's paradise.

Look to the east to Main Tickle and watch for whales and grounded icebergs in the summer months. The trail continues north along the

Distance:
6.5-kilometre linear trail

Trailhead: Horwood Lane
(49.392905, -54.435889)

Highlights: Rugged coastline, geology, beaches

Elev. range: 0–60 metres

coast. Hug the shoreline if the path is overgrown or unclear in places. At Spiller's Cove you can decide to take the trail leading back to Durrell or continue on to make a longer loop hike and include Spiller's Cove to French Beach.

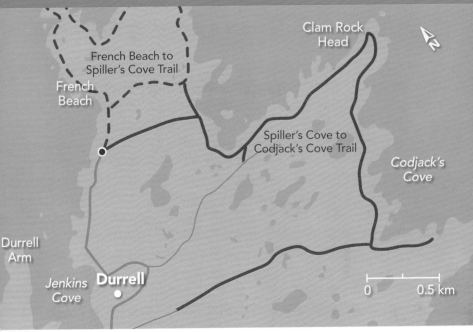

Trail maps are **not to be used for navigation.**

 Codjack, according to local historians, is a codfish. The Spanish that fished off Newfoundland named it *bacalao*, after which Baccalieu Island was named. Many Newfoundlanders refer to cod as simply "fish" as it was the most common fish caught and eaten in the province.

Little Harbour

This delightful loop trail starts in Little Harbour on the east side of the island of Twillingate.

The community of Lower Cove was resettled when Newfoundland joined Canada in 1949. Part of the Confederation agreement was that all children in the new province must attend school, which forced whole families to move.

Lower Cove was also the winter residence of Thomas Sugg, who lived to be 110, one of the longest living Newfoundlanders.

The trail winds through various vegetation zones; the spongy peat-covered section of the trail is especially welcoming to weary feet. As with many headland trails in the area, there are several lookout points or smaller offshoot trails that all lead back to the main trail.

A large abandoned root cellar of the Keefe family from the 1930s is found along the way. This trail showcases fascinating geology and no examples are more prominent than the 30-metre-high sea arch and, close by it, the magma dike along the shoreline which reveals the volcanic activity that formed the region.

The trail winds along the coast until it reaches beautiful Jones Cove and then heads back overland to complete the loop.

> ★ Magma dikes are formed from igneous rock. Igneous rock is formed after magma, a hot semi-liquid substance that exists below the earth's crust, cools and eventually becomes solid. Pressure and heat in the earth's core can force magmatic material through fractures in the earth's crust and make them visible in rock outcrops.

Distance: 5.5-kilometre loop

Trailhead: Lower Little Harbour (49.373985, -54.423414)

Highlights: Resettled community, sea arch, magma dike

Elev. range: 0–46 metres

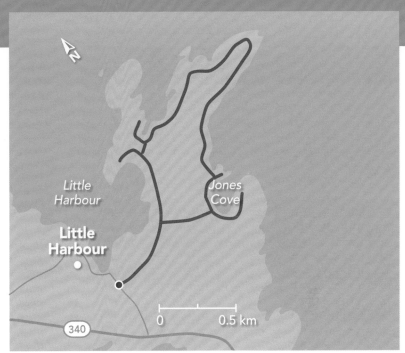

Little
Harbour

Jones
Cove

**Little
Harbour**

340

0   0.5 km

Trail maps are **not to be used for navigation.**

The Burin Peninsula is a large appendage jutting southward into the North Atlantic from the island of Newfoundland. It is a magical place steeped in history, tragedy, and natural beauty. The towns and communities are sparsely inhabited and much of the coastline is not accessible by car.

By road, the peninsula is accessed from the Trans-Canada Highway by turning onto Highway 210 at Goobies. Swift Current is the first community strung along the highway. The next major community is Marystown, 122 kilometres to the southwest. The landscape changes dramatically as you travel south: thick forest with spruce and deciduous trees turns to large open tracts of low-growing shrubs and rock. Carry an emergency kit in your vehicle as fog and potholes could leave you on a lonely highway with little traffic for a long time.

Several side roads end at tiny communities that are well worth a stop— Bay L'Argent, Petite Forte, Rushoon, and Red Harbour, among others. At Marystown, the vistas change dramatically again, from hilly barrens to the ocean and a prosperous community where the main industry is a shipyard and fabrication facility that primarily services the province's offshore industry.

We made our first stop in the historic town of Burin for a stroll around Salt Pond. Burin has several picturesque sheltered coves, once used by rum-runners, which can be clearly seen at the base of high cliffs from Captain Cook Lookout. You can imagine pirates and privateers of bygone times sailing between hidden coves with contraband rum bought from nearby St. Pierre.

St. Lawrence is a community at the "heel" of the peninsula. Cap Chapeau Rouge looms to the southeast of Great St. Lawrence Harbour. St. Lawrence has its share of history, fame, and prosperity, including the 1942 sinking of the *Pollux* and *Truxton*. On the way to Fortune, small com-

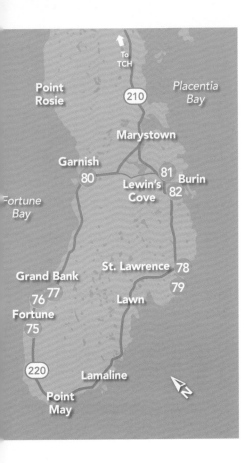

munities—Lawn, Roundabout, Calmer, and others—dot the shoreline. The French islands of St. Pierre and Miquelon can be seen on a clear day offshore from the "toe" of the peninsula.

Grand Bank wears its history well in its architecture alone. Queen-Anne-style homes topped with widow walks once owned by sea captains and wealthy merchants still stand proudly and make for great photo opportunities.

Finish the loop by heading north to Garnish. From a vantage point on the Long Ridge Trail, Garnish appears as a tidy small community surrounded by startling coastal beauty. From there the road veers east once again to take you back to Marystown.

Burin Trails

75. Horse Brook Trail / Fortune
76. Marine Trail / Grand Bank
77. Nature Trail / Grand Bank
78. The Cape Trail / St. Lawrence
79. Chambers Cove Trail / St. Lawrence
80. Long Ridge Trail / Garnish
81. Salt Pond Walking Trail / Burin
82. Captain Cook Lookout / Burin

Fortune

Although Fortune is known as the jumping-off point for travellers taking the ferry to the French islands of St. Pierre and Miquelon, this historic town has much to offer in its own right. The Fortune Head Ecological Reserve is one of only three sites in the world where the transition from the pre-Cambrian to the Cambrian era is evident in the fossil record. It is also home to the Horse Brook Trail, a pleasant walking path.

Walkers can access this trail either at the Horsebrook Trailer Park just off Eldon Street or from Hornhouse Road.

Horse Brook Trail is a gentle amble along the banks of Horse Brook.

Where boardwalks were necessary, they were well built but, due to flooding, some have shifted from their footings and are a little off-kilter. Otherwise, the path is in good shape.

Horse Brook is a quiet, pretty little river for most of the year, but it is evident from erosion along its banks that it can present a different picture when water levels are high. An abundance of wildflowers grows along the riverbank in season and in late August expect a rich harvest from the many chokecherry trees.

You could leave a vehicle at either end of the trail, but as the trail is so short it makes sense to walk both ways.

Chokecherry is a member of the Rose family. The fruit is sweet, easily recognizable by its long stems (similar to those of cherries), and easy to pick. The berries are dark purple or red when ripe and have a large pit that becomes soft and edible when cooked. Chokecherries are ripe in late August to early September and are known by a variety of names: chuckley pears, shadberries, chuck, serviceberries, wild pears, juneberries, chockly plums, Indian pears, and Saskatoon berries.

Distance:
2-kilometre linear trail

Trailhead: Hornhouse Road (47.031630, -55.503550); Horsebrook Trailer Park 47.034982, -55.495855)

Highlights: River, wildflowers, chokecherry trees

Elev. range: 7–16 metres

Trail maps are **not to be used for navigation.**

Grand Bank

Marine Trail begins at the end of College Street in the town of Grand Bank. Walk across the beach that separates Admiral Cove Pond from the ocean and then climb to the top of the cape. From this vantage point, the town is spread out like a giant map.

To the east is Fortune. To the north, in the middle of Fortune Bay, is Brunette Island, where an attempt to develop a bison herd in 1964 proved unsuccessful.

The path is easy to follow as it continues across the open headland and then traces the coastline toward Fortune. On a clear day, it is possible to see the French islands of St. Pierre and Miquelon. You can imagine that the headland was also a spot where people walked and waited anxiously, looking for signs of local mariners reportedly lost at sea.

> ⭐ Several large homes in Grand Bank have a widow's walk, also called a widow's watch—a railed roof walkway on a platform, often enclosed in a small cupola, at the top of a house. Some say the widow's walks were designed for women who were mourning for husbands who did not return from their sea journeys.

Distance:
7-kilometre linear trail

Trailhead: College Street, Grand Bank (47.060817, -55.454829); Eternity Rock, Grand Bank-Fortune highway (47.052829, -55.472842)

Highlights: Views of Grand Bank, coastline

Elev. range: 0–47 metres

Eventually the trail leads to L'Anse au Paul Beach. Partway down the beach, take the road that turns east and leads out to the Grand Bank-Fortune highway. Turn left at the highway and proceed along the road to the trail's end at Eternity Rock. If you don't have a vehicle waiting, walk back along the road to Grand Bank, or retrace your steps over the trail.

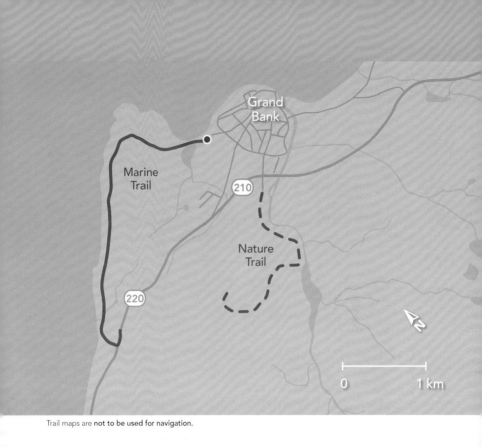

Marine Trail

Grand Bank

210

220

Nature Trail

0   1 km

Trail maps are **not to be used for navigation.**

Grand Bank

Farmer's Hill Road in Grand Bank leads to the beginning of the Nature Trail. The path follows along the bank of Grand Bank Brook and quickly arrives at a dam and fish ladder. Beyond the brook, you will enter thick woods and eventually arrive at a gazebo on Simms Ridge for an impressive view of the town and ocean. Scotch pines planted on this hillside by the local Boy Scout troop in the 1950s are an interesting

alternative to the usual fare in a Newfoundland forest.

From the gazebo, you will head toward a high communications tower. The path proceeds to Bennett's Hill Lookout and another outstanding view of the town below. From this lookout you can descend the hill to the main road or return the way you came to Farmer's Hill Road.

New trail infrastructure includes a picnic area and two lookouts. The path is generally in good condition but there is an absence of signs and, because of intersecting roads and trails, the trail can be confusing. A good signboard with a map of the trail would be helpful.

 Because of its proximity to the rich fishing banks offshore, Grand Bank was a prosperous harbour as early as the 1880s. Schooners built here to ply the waters were called Grand Bankers.

Distance:
6-kilometre linear trail

Trailhead: Farmer's Hill Road
(47.053558, -55.454392);
Grandview Boulevard,
(47.052688, -55.472661)

Highlights: Views of Grand Bank and coast, forest vegetation

Elev. range: 6–79 metres

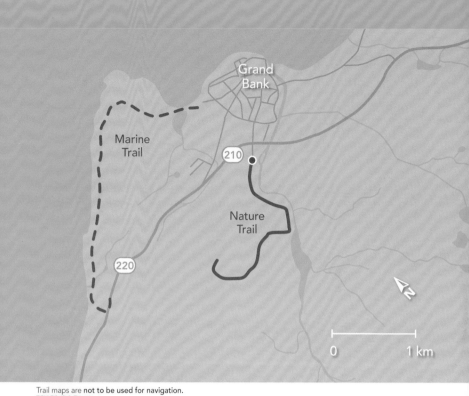

Trail maps are **not to be used for navigation.**

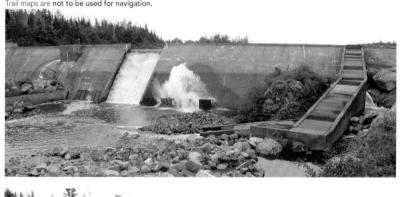

179

78 THE CAPE TRAIL (CAP CHAPEAU ROUGE)

St. Lawrence

As you follow Pollux Crescent on the west side of St. Lawrence out of the town, the pavement soon gives way to gravel. A short way along the road is the clearly marked start to the Cape Trail that goes to the summit of Cap Chapeau Rouge.

This trail has two distinct elements: the flat section and the steep section. For the first few kilometres, the path winds through woods and then across an open bog before a steep ascent to the top of the cape.

There is some plank infrastructure but take care on old boardwalk that is not in the best of condition. The path is often wet and muddy in places.

The climb to the top can be challenging as the trail is rocky and steep. This is one of the highest points on the Burin Peninsula and the views are impressive—worth the ascent. From here, you can look down the bay to the town of St. Lawrence; in the other direction Chambers Cove and Lawn Head are easily visible.

It is always windy on top of the cape and can be foggy, so be prepared. Return via the same trail.

Distance:
4-kilometre linear trail

Trailhead: Pollux Crescent, St. Lawrence (46.542527, -55.233923)

Highlights: Bog vegetation, views from summit

Elev. range: 30–211 metres

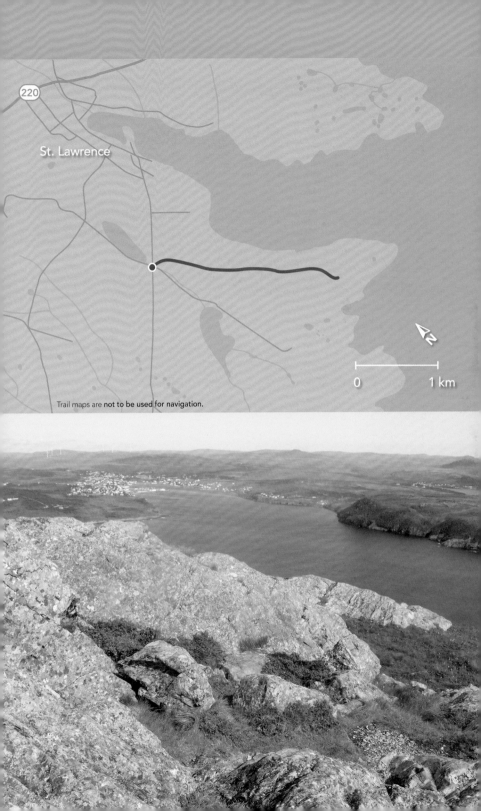

220

St. Lawrence

Trail maps are **not to be used for navigation.**

N

0   1 km

St. Lawrence

Chambers Cove near St. Lawrence would be just one of many scenic coves and bays around Newfoundland were it not for the events of November 18, 1942. On that night, three US Navy vessels ran aground in Chambers Cove and on nearby Lawn Head. Although 203 American sailors died that night, 186 were rescued by the heroic efforts of local residents.

This trail begins at the end of Iron Spring Road, an extension of Pollux Crescent in St. Lawrence. This multi-

use trail is used by ATVs as well as walkers, at least as far as Salt Cove. There, by the small hay shed where several of the first men up the cliff took shelter in 1942, a long stairway leads to the top of the cliff looking down on Chambers Cove.

The USS *Truxton* ran aground in this cove, the USS *Pollux* and USS *Wilkes* farther west on Lawn Head. Signboards explain the events of that historic night.

Hikers may wander freely on the open headland and admire the beauty of this stretch of coast, which is characterized by both dangerous rocky cliffs and sandy beaches. When you are ready to return, take the Bergeron Path by way of Salt Cove, the route taken by Seaman Ed Bergeron, the first survivor to make it ashore and who alerted men at the Iron Spring Mine of the disaster. This path brings you back to the car park at the trailhead.

> ⭐ *Standing into Danger,* by Cassie Brown, recounts the true story of the *Truxton* and *Pollux* sinkings, one of the worst disasters in Newfoundland's naval history.

Distance:
4-kilometre loop trail

Trailhead: Iron Spring Road, St. Lawrence (46.530277, -55.251273)

Highlights: Coastal scenery, historical significance

Elev. range: 7–60 metres

220

Great St. Lawrence Harbour

Shoal Cove

Ferryland Head

Chambers Cove Trail

Chambers Point

N

0   1 km

Trail maps are **not to be used for navigation**.

Garnish

The trailhead for the Long Ridge Trail is on the right side of Sunset Drive as you enter Garnish from Frenchman's Cove. Watch for the sign by the trail entrance; parking is located a few metres farther down the road, on the ocean side.

Distance: 1.8-kilometre linear trail (4 kilometres, including town walk)

Trailhead: Sunset Drive, Garnish (47.134290, -55.223065); Salvation Army Cemetery (47.134201, -55.214725)

Highlights: Views from the ridge, harbour walk

Elev. range: 1–72 metres

It doesn't take long for this path to offer hikers beautiful rewards. As you make your way toward the ridge, the thick forest begins to thin and, at the first viewpoint, the path reveals a panoramic view of the coast. At Frenchman's Cove to the southwest you can see the long crescent beach creating a barachois behind it, and the man-made rolling greens of a nine-hole golf course. In the opposite direction is the town of Garnish with its secure little harbour and marina.

From the 70-metre peak, the trail descends back into thick forest, eventually emerging at the Salvation Army Cemetery at the northeast end of town. You could have a second car waiting there, but a better idea is to walk back through town, taking Barrisway Street to Waterfront Road by the harbour. Seaview Drive will lead you back to Sunset Drive and the trailhead.

The infrastructure, upgraded in 2011, is in good condition.

An interesting fact from a storyboard in Garnish: Philip and Charles Grandy, born on Jersey in the British Channel Islands, were the first to settle here, having been forced out of the French island of St. Pierre, just off the Burin Peninsula, in 1763. "Garnish" is believed to have derived from the word "Cornish," the original ancestral home of these early settlers.

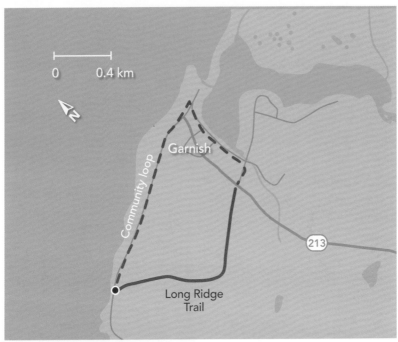

Trail maps are **not to be used for navigation.**

Burin

Salt Pond is located beside Main Street as you approach Burin from Marystown. The pond empties southwest into Burin Bay Arm via a narrow channel under a bridge on Eagle Road. Salt Pond Walking Trail is a gentle 2.5-kilometre walk circling the pond and is suitable for all ages. It can easily be completed in 30 to 40 minutes.

The boardwalk and crushed-stone walkway passes at times through lush forest and, at other times, weaves its way between houses and the pond edge. Look for a wide array of wildflowers and wildlife, including ospreys hovering above the water trying to catch a fish for dinner. Walkers are almost certain to encounter a large covey of ducks near the footbridge.

The infrastructure on this walk is well built and appears to undergo regular maintenance. Viewing benches and picnic tables are provided and the dock on the west side of the pond is an especially good place to stop and picnic or just to enjoy the peace and tranquility of this area.

Distance: 2.5-kilometre loop

Trailhead: Salt Pond, Main Street (47.055703, -55.115257)

Highlights: Birds, wildflowers, pond

Elev. range: 1–20 metres

Salt
Pond

220

222

To
Burin

221

0   0.3 km

Trail maps are **not to be used** for navigation.

Burin

This trail begins at the end of Penney's Pond Road just off Main Street on the approach to Burin. A boardwalk and stairways added in recent years have greatly improved this trail.

After passing by Penney's Pond, the trail takes hikers through thick coniferous woods and then descends to near sea level before climbing to

⭐ **James Cook**, the famous Royal Navy explorer and cartographer for whom this trail is named, mapped the coastline around Newfoundland in the mid-18th century. He subsequently mapped Australia and New Zealand and circumnavigated the globe three times before being killed in an altercation with Hawaiian natives in 1779.

Distance: 3-kilometre linear trail (6-kilometre return)

Trailhead: Penney's Pond Road, Burin (47.022165, -55.103678)

Highlights: Magnificent views from the lookout

Elev. range: 6–75 metres

the 75-metre-high lookout. The trail is more rugged on the climb, so be careful, especially in wet conditions.

In the 18th century, this lookout provided an ideal vantage point from which to spot smugglers or the approaching pirates or privateers who periodically raided coastal settlements. You can peer down from the lookout onto fishing boats docked in Epworth, and across the bay you will see Burin and its waterfront boardwalk. Burin Inlet is picturesque and dotted with islands of all shapes and sizes.

Return to the trailhead by the same path.

Burin

Burin
Inlet

Collins
Cove

Ship
Cove

N

0   0.4 km

Trail maps are **not to be used for navigation.**

WILDERNESS TRAILS

We have identified these hikes as wilderness trails for a few reasons: signage may or may not exist; they feature little or no infrastructure; and/or existing infrastructure has deteriorated and no maintenance is planned.

The Outport Trail in Terra Nova National Park has been designated a wilderness trail not because of a lack of will or ability to maintain it but because it offers the hiker a vastly different experience from shorter, more easily accessible park trails. Hikers along this trail are more likely to encounter wildlife than fellow human beings. It also offers unsupervised campsites far removed from the more heavily used sites in the Newman Sound campground.

These trails demand more from the hiker than those in other sections of this book. In some cases, hikers are requested to register with the builder/sponsor (explained in the individual hike descriptions) before setting out. In the case of the Wreck Path, hikers are strongly advised to check with the East Coast Trail Association and find out if a guided hike of the route is planned.

The Old Trails from Sandy Cove to Salvage is a one-day hike. The other three wilderness hikes take at least two days to complete. For those, be prepared for a little more physical challenge. The excitement of being in a place rarely seen by others, the increased likelihood of encountering wildlife, and the feeling of discovery are ample reward for the extra effort expended.

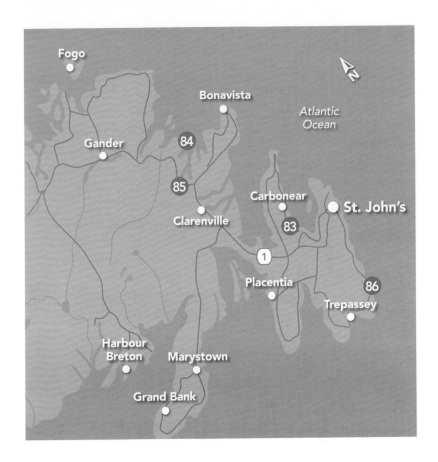

Wilderness Trails

Makinsons to Hopeall

Established in 1612 to foster a fur trade with the Beothuk Indians, this trail, which may be the oldest in Newfoundland, was reopened in 1997 by the Baccalieu Trail Heritage Corporation.

Originally, Crout's Way crossed the Bay de Verde Peninsula from Cupids to Hopeall. Its new trailhead is by a heritage farmhouse in Drogheda, a few kilometres west of Clarke's Beach along the South River Road.

This 35-kilometre two-day hike can be broken into smaller segments, as it crosses several roads, including Veteran's Memorial Highway. It covers a variety of terrains and fairly steep climbs, especially in the first part of the trail leaving Drogheda.

At roughly the halfway point the trail arrives at the "old track," the former railbed that crosses the New Harbour-Tilton barrens. This is a potential pickup and drop-off site as the track is well-used by cabin owners. There is also some level ground here on which to set up a tent.

Shortly after leaving the old track you will catch your first glimpse of Trinity Bay—the same view Crout mentioned in his journal. The trail eventually passes between Sutton's Pond and Island Pond and then along the riverbank into Hopeall.

Although some signage may be found on the trail, this is not always an easy path to follow; a good topographical map is essential. The Crossroads for Cultures website (www.crossroadsforcultures.ca) provides a description of Crout's route with links to his journal.

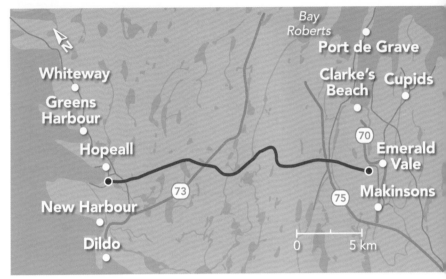

Trail maps are not to be used for navigation.

 John Guy, the founder of the Cupers Cove Colony (now Cupids), commissioned Henry Crout to cut a trail from the Colony to Mount Eagle Bay (now Hopeall) in Trinity Bay to make contact with the Aboriginal peoples and foster a fur trade. Good relations were not established with the Beothuks, and the trail was never used as intended.

Distance: 35-kilometre linear trail

Trailheads: Drogheda R.V. Park (from the TCH heading west turn onto Route 71; at South River Road turn left to the Drogheda R.V. Park, 47.303643, -53.181107)

Hopeall (park by the bridge over Hopeall River; a large sign marks the trailhead, 47.363040, -53.305398)

Highlights: Rivers, ponds, hilltop views

Elev. range: 0–155 metres

Sandy Cove to Salvage

This 14-kilometre trail linking two Eastport Peninsula communities is actually a series of old trails that were traditionally used by berry pickers, hunters, and woodcutters. This inland trail features a varied terrain and viewpoints that look out onto Newman Sound.

The Eastport Peninsula Heritage

Society reopened the trails in 1997 and joined them to form a continuous pathway.

Beginning from Crooked Tree Park in Sandy Cove, the trail climbs steadily through thick woods and eventually emerges onto a bald ridge. It passes a series of ponds on both sides of the path before entering thick woods once again.

A brochure with a map of this trail is available at The Beaches Heritage Centre in Eastport. The eight individual trails that constitute the Old Trails have been delineated and described. The Heritage Society requests that people check in at the Centre before beginning this hike.

Windfalls covered the path when we hiked it in 2013 and it was difficult to find the way through in some places. Waterproof footwear is a must for muddy sections.

Eventually the trail circles halfway around Lind's Pond (48.394900, -53.393042) before climbing toward the barrens and a view overlooking a fjord at Broomclose.

Distance:
14-kilometre linear trail

Trailheads: Crooked Tree Park, Sandy Cove (48.411002, -53.384284); Fisherman's Museum, Salvage (48.383261, -53.433930)

Highlights: Panoramic view, ponds, waterfall

Elev. range: 7–171 metres

The final section of trail passes through an area called the Meshes and winds its way into Salvage.

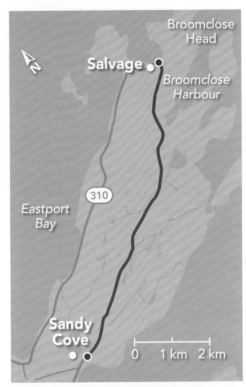

Broomclose
Head

Salvage

Broomclose
Harbour

310

Eastport
Bay

Sandy
Cove

0   1 km 2 km

Trail maps are **not to be used for** navigation.

Terra Nova National Park

Terra Nova National Park has many walking trails, but, if you are looking for a wilderness experience, the Outport Trail will remove you from most of the trappings of civilization.

Leaving the Newman Sound Campground, the trail passes around the muddy flats of the

sound and follows the coastline in an easterly direction. Eleven kilometres along the path a side trail leads to the summit of Mount Stamford. The highest point in the park, it offers a panoramic view.

Approximately 3 kilometres farther is the campsite at Minchin Cove, where there is a boat dock. Contact Coastal Connections at Salton's Brook about a drop-off at Minchin Cove if you prefer to hike only one-way. There is no supervision at this campsite, nor at those at South Broad Cove and Lion's Den North and South. The trail is maintained only as far as South Broad Cove.

The secluded beauty of Minchin Cove makes it an ideal overnight spot, but this is black bear territory—store food on bear poles and pack out all garbage. Hikers and campers must register with the park office.

★ Minchin Cove is named for the Minchin family, who kept a fishing camp there in the 1800s. A sawmill, later built on the site, was operated successfully by the King family until the mid-20th century. Old mill equipment is still in evidence around the cove.

Distance: 14-kilometre linear trail to Minchin Cove; 22-kilometre linear trail to Lion's Den South

Trailhead: Site 253, Newman Sound campground (48.322118, -53.581801)

Highlights: Boreal forest, beaver pond, Mount Stamford, Minchin Cove

Elev. range: 1–150 metres

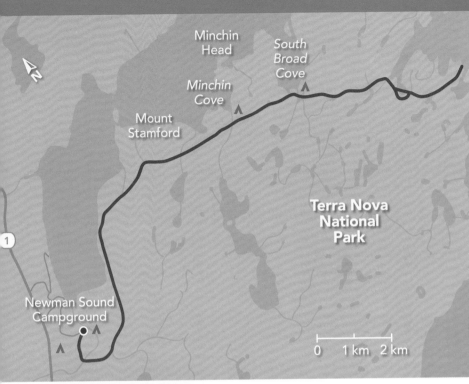

Minchin
Head

South
Broad
Cove

Minchin
Cove

Mount
Stamford

Terra Nova
National
Park

Newman Sound
Campground

0   1 km   2 km

Trail maps are **not to be used** for navigation.

Cappahayden to Cape Race

This route from Cappahayden to Cape Race is an extension of the East Coast Trail; because it has never been developed and is not properly flagged, it should not be attempted alone. We strongly recommend that anyone who wants to do this 35-kilometre two-day hike should contact the East Coast Trail office and inquire about ECTA guided hikes on this path.

The path is named for the many shipwrecks that have occurred along this stretch of coast, including the *Florizel* in 1918. Sections of the trail follow the clifftops but extended sections across large barrens have few if any markings and difficult footing. Expect to encounter numerous fallen trees in wooded sections.

Distance:
35-kilometre linear trail

Trailheads: Cappahayden
(46.513833, -52.564216);
Cape Race Lighthouse
(46.395108, -53.042665)

Highlights: Coastal views, spectacular barrens, wildlife

Elev. range: 0–113 metres

The halfway point is Chance Cove Provincial Park, where there is a river to carefully ford before setting up tents for the night.

On day two, the path leads beside Clam Cove, where the SS *Anglo-Saxon* went down in 1863. With the loss of 237 lives, it was the worst shipping disaster in Newfoundland history.

A long trek across the expansive Cape Race barrens leads to the lighthouse at Cape Race. On April 14, 1912, the lighthouse keeper helped to coordinate the rescue effort by the SS *Carpathia* and other vessels for the world's most famous ill-fated luxury liner, the SS *Titanic*.

This challenging path is not without its rewards. In addition to the stunning views, coastal and inland, wild-life sightings are almost a certainty: watch for moose, caribou, and seals.

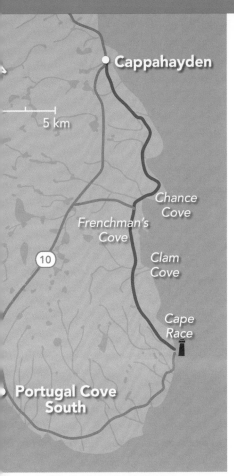

Cappahayden

5 km

Chance
Cove

Frenchman's
Cove

Clam
Cove

Cape
Race

10

Portugal Cove
South

Trail maps are **not to be used for navigation.**

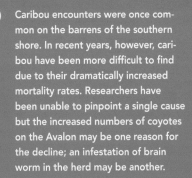

Caribou encounters were once common on the barrens of the southern shore. In recent years, however, caribou have been more difficult to find due to their dramatically increased mortality rates. Researchers have been unable to pinpoint a single cause but the increased numbers of coyotes on the Avalon may be one reason for the decline; an infestation of brain worm in the herd may be another.

Wildflowers of eastern Newfoundland

As you walk or hike the trails of eastern Newfoundland, particularly in the summer months, look for these and other wildflowers. Below are photographs of just some of the more frequently spotted wildflowers; also included is each species' common name, Latin name, flowering period, and habitat.

Bering sea chickweed
Cerastium beeringianum
Flowers: May to September
Habitat: Gravel roadsides

Bird's-eye primrose
Primula laurentiana
Flowers: June to August
Habitat: Rocky areas, shorelines

Blue flag
Iris versicolor
Flowers: July
Habitat: Wetlands, bogs

Crackerberry (bunchberry)
Cornus canadensis
Flowers: White flower in July,
red clustered berries in September
Habitat: Forest trails

Creeping buttercup
Ranunculus repens
Flowers: May to August
Habitat: Wet areas, ditches

Fireweed
Epilobium angustifolium
Flowers: July to August
Habitat: Clearings, burned-over areas

Grass pink
Calopogon tuberosus
Flowers: July and August
Habitat: Boggy areas

Harebell
Campanula rotundifolia
Flowers: June to September
Habitat: Meadows, grassy areas

Labrador tea
Rhododendron groenlandicum
Flowers: July and August
Habitat: Bogs, fens, woodlands

Lupin
Lupines polyphyllus
Flowers: July
Habitat: Ditches, clearings, roadsides

Marsh marigold
Caltha palustris
Flowers: June
Habitat: Wet areas

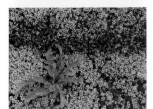

Moss campion
Silene acaulis
Flowers: July
Habitat: Hilltops, coastal cliffs

Musk mallow
Malva moschata
Flowers: June to September
Habitat: Fields, roadsides

One-flowered wintergreen
Moneses uniflora
Flowers: July and August
Habitat: Forests, bogs

Orange hawkweed (devil's paintbrush)
Hieracium aurantiacum
Flowers: June to September
Habitat: Roadsides, fields

Oxeye daisy
Chrysanthemum leucanthemum
Flowers: June to August
Habitat: Roadsides, fields

Pearly everlasting
Anaphalis margaritacea
Flowers: July to September
Habitat: Gravel roadsides, pastures

Pink lady's-slipper
Cypripedium acaule
Flowers: May and June
Habitat: Wet areas, woods

Pitcher plant
Sarracenia purpurea
Flowers: May and June
Habitat: Sphagnum bogs

Roseroot
Sedum rosea
Flowers: June and July
Habitat: Rocky coastal areas

Rough-leaved aster
Aster radula
Flowers: July to September
Habitat: Wet woodlands, stream borders

Sheep laurel
Kalmia angustifolia
Flowers: Late June to July
Habitat: Various acidic habitats

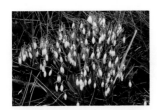

Snowdrop
Galanthus nivalis
Flowers: April to May
Habitat: Wet woodlands

Starflower
Trientalis borealis
Flowers: May and June
Habitat: Woodlands, high slopes

Three-toothed cinquefoil
Potentilla tridentata
Flowers: June to August
Habitat: Acidic soil, rocky areas

Twinflower
Linnaea borealis
Flowers: June to August
Habitat: Coniferous forest, alpine barrens

Wild rose (wrinkled rose)
Rosa rugosa
Flowers: July to August
Habitat: Various habitats

Trail Completion Checklist

Avalon Peninsula

- ❏ Trails of Signal Hill
- ❏ Butter Pot Hill Trail
- ❏ Grates Cove Trails
- ❏ Sea View Trail
- ❏ d'Iberville Trail
- ❏ Brigus Lighthouse Trail
- ❏ Burnt Head Trail
- ❏ Blackhead to Western Bay
- ❏ Bay Roberts Shoreline Heritage Walk
- ❏ Bordeaux Trail
- ❏ Bird Rock
- ❏ St. Mary's to Gaskiers
- ❏ Gregory Normore Walking Trail

East Coast Trail

- ❏ Picco's Ridge Path
- ❏ White Horse Path
- ❏ Biscan Cove Path
- ❏ Stiles Cove Path
- ❏ Father Troy's Trail
- ❏ Silver Mine Head Path
- ❏ Cobbler Path
- ❏ Sugarloaf Path
- ❏ Deadmans Bay Path
- ❏ Blackhead Path
- ❏ Cape Spear Path
- ❏ Motion Path
- ❏ Spout Path
- ❏ Mickeleens Path
- ❏ Beaches Path
- ❏ Tinkers Point Path
- ❏ La Manche Village Path
- ❏ Flamber Head Path

- ❏ Brigus Head Path
- ❏ Cape Broyle Head Path
- ❏ Caplin Bay Path
- ❏ Sounding Hills Path
- ❏ Mudder Wet Path
- ❏ Spurwink Island Path
- ❏ Bear Cove Point Path
- ❏ Island Meadow Path

Bonavista Peninsula

- ❏ Centre Hill Trail
- ❏ Truce Sound Peace Garden Trail
- ❏ Bare Mountain Trail
- ❏ Rotary/Wellness Trails
- ❏ Shoal Harbour Loop
- ❏ Dungeon to Cape Bonavista
- ❏ Klondike Trail
- ❏ Little Catalina to Maberly Trail
- ❏ Lodge's Pond to Murphy's Cove Trail
- ❏ Fox Island Trail
- ❏ Skerwink Trail
- ❏ British Harbour Trail
- ❏ King's Cove Lighthouse Trail

All around the Circle: Road to the Shore
Fogo Island, Change Islands, and Twillingate

Road to the Shore

- ❏ Middle Brook River Trail
- ❏ Greenspond Island Trail
- ❏ Cape Island Walking Trail

Fogo Island

- ❑ Deep Bay
- ❑ Waterman's Brook Trail
- ❑ Brimstone Head Trail
- ❑ Fogo Head Trail
- ❑ Lion's Den Trail
- ❑ Shoal Bay Trail
- ❑ Great Auk Trail
- ❑ Turpin's Trail West
- ❑ Turpin's Trail East
- ❑ Oliver's Cove Footpath

Change Islands

- ❑ Squid Jigger Trail
- ❑ Shoreline Path
- ❑ Salt Water Pond Loop
- ❑ Indian Lookout

Twillingate

- ❑ Lower Head Loop
- ❑ Sleepy Cove Trail
- ❑ French Beach to Spiller's Cove Trail
- ❑ Spiller's Cove to Codjack's Cove Trail
- ❑ Lower Little Harbour Trail

Burin Peninsula

- ❑ Horse Brook Trail
- ❑ Marine Trail
- ❑ Nature Trail
- ❑ The Cape Trail (Cap Chapeau Rouge)
- ❑ Chambers Cove Trail
- ❑ Long Ridge Trail
- ❑ Salt Pond Walking Trail
- ❑ Captain Cook Lookout

Wilderness Trails

- ❑ Crout's Way
- ❑ The Old Trails
- ❑ The Outport Trail
- ❑ Wreck Path

References

Bruneau, Stephen E. *Icebergs of Newfoundland and Labrador*. St. John's: Flanker Press, 2004.

Burrows, Roger. *Birds of Atlantic Canada*. Edmonton: Lone Pine Publishing, 2002.

Coleman-Sadd, Stephen and Susan A. Scott. *Newfoundland and Labrador: Traveller's Guide to the Geology*. St. John's: Geological Association of Canada, Newfoundland Section, 1994.

Dawe, Corrina M. and Robert H. Cuff. *Walker's Handbook, Grand Concourse*. St. John's: The Johnson Family Foundation, 1999.

Gard, Peter, ed. *Hiking the East Coast Trail—Fort Amherst to Petty Harbour/ Maddox Cove*. St. John's: East Coast Trail Association, 2001.

——. *Hiking the East Coast Trail—Petty Harbour/Maddox Cove to Bay Bulls*. St. John's: East Coast Trail Association, 2005.

Hennebury, Andy, Lynette Adams, and Marc Poirier. *Hiking on the Discovery Trail: A Guide to Hiking on the Bonavista Peninsula*. Clarenville: The Discovery Trail Tourism Association, 2002.

Hild, Martha Hickman. *Geology of Newfoundland*. Portugal Cove-St. Philip's: Boulder Publications, 2012.

Mellin, Robert. *Tilting: House Launching, Slide Hauling, Potato Trenching and Other Tales from a Newfoundland Fishing Village*. New York: Princeton Architectural Press, 2003.

Peterson, Roger Tory and Margaret McKenny. *A Field Guide to Wildflowers of Northeastern and North-central North America*. Boston: Houghton Mifflin Company, 1968.

Scott, Peter J. *Wildflowers of Newfoundland and Labrador*. Portugal Cove-St. Philip's: Boulder Publications, 2008.

——. *Edible Plants of Newfoundland and Labrador*. Portugal Cove-St. Philip's: Boulder Publications, 2010.

Smyth, Mary and Fred Hollingshurst. *52 Great Hikes: Newfoundland and Labrador*. Conception Bay South: WCYi Publishing, 2005.

Story, G.M., W.J. Kirwin, and J.D.A. Widdowson. *Dictionary of Newfoundland English*. 2nd. ed. Toronto: University of Toronto Press, 1999.

Titford, Bill and June Titford. *A Traveller's Guide to Wild Flowers of Newfoundland Canada*. St. John's: Flora Frames, 1995.

Useful websites

East Coast Trail Association: for information about the East Coast Trail, planned hikes, and official East Coast Trail map packages: www.eastcoasttrail.com

Newfoundland and Labrador Department of Tourism, Culture and Recreation: www.newfoundlandlabrador.com

Newfoundland and Labrador Ferry Schedules: www.tw.gov.nl.ca/ferryservices/schedules

Marine Atlantic Ferry Service: www.marine-atlantic.ca

Newfoundland Pony Sanctuary (Change Islands) www.nlponysanctuary.com

Newfoundland and Labrador Provincial Parks and Cape St. Mary's Ecological Reserve: www.env.gov.nl.ca/env/parks/parks/find

Parks Canada (Parks and National Historic Sites): www.pc.ca

The Grand Concourse: trails within St. John's and neighbouring communities: www.grandconcourse.ca

Natural Resources Canada: www.atlas.nrcan.gc.ca/site/english/toporama

Photo credits

All photographs in this book are by Mary Smyth or Fred Hollingshurst, with these exceptions:

Fraser Carpenter: Turpin's Trail East (yellow legs)

Darlene Scott: Deadman's Path (barachois beach), La Manche (harbour view), Spout Path (spout), Bear Cove (wildflowers)

Garry Smyth: Cobbler Brook Path (drone photo view south to Cobbler Brook)

INDEX BY HIKE DIFFICULTY

The numbers that appear by the hike names refer to hike numbers, not page numbers.

INDEX BY PLACE NAME

The numbers that appear by hike names refer to hike numbers, not page numbers.

About the Authors

Mary Smyth was raised in the east end of St. John's in a large boisterous family. She fondly remembers summer picnic expeditions to the beautiful coves, beaches, and meadows of her parents' beloved Southern Shore. The seed for her love of the outdoors grew from there; a degree in physical geography enhanced her under-standing and appreciation of the natural world. On her return from 25 years of living in Europe, she worked with the provincial tourism association and tourism operators in the province to develop standards for the adventure tourism industry. It was an opportunity to become more deeply acquainted with this incredible part of the world.

Fred Hollingshurst caught the hiking bug when, fresh out of university, he spent a year tramping around Europe and North Africa. Originally from British Columbia, he has made Newfoundland and Labrador home since 1968. He worked briefly for NTV and the *Daily News* before settling into a long career as a producer with Memorial University's Educational Television Centre. Travel through work and pleasure has enabled him to explore many regions in this beautiful province. He has also been wilderness backpacking in British Columbia in bear country and has guided hiking groups on the East Coast Trail.

Mary and Fred wrote a hiking column, *Along the Trail*, for the *Telegram* for nine years. Their first hiking book, *52 Great Hikes*, was published in 2005. Together they have hiked all of the East Coast Trail and many of the trails of western and central Newfoundland. They have also had the extreme pleasure of hiking in the Torngat Mountains National Park in Labrador. They have been granted their "Compostela" after an 800-kilometre pilgrimage on the Camino in Northern Spain, crossed England on the Coast to Coast Trail, and hiked the Cinque Terra in Liguria, Italy. They live and garden in Outer Cove, Newfoundland.